Voice
Hollers

Voice for the Hollers

A Journey Into Solitude and Solidarity in Appalachia

Jeanne McNulty

Outskirts Press, Inc.
Denver, Colorado

Voice for the Hollers
A Journey Into Solitude and Solidarity in Appalachia
All Rights Reserved.
Copyright © 2010 Jeanne McNulty
v2.0 r1.0

Outskirts Press, Inc.
http://www.outskirtspress.com

ISBN: 978-1-4327-4534-9

Outskirts Press and the "OP" logo are trademarks belonging to Outskirts Press, Inc.

PRINTED IN THE UNITED STATES OF AMERICA

Contents

CHAPTER 1

Ashby Franklin "Jack" Tanner

"'Tis the gift to be simple, 'Tis the gift to be free, 'Tis the gift to come down where we ought to be." Simple Gifts, Shaker Song.

Jack stood there, his feet firmly planted on my rickety front porch exclaiming: "I just can't see why you cannot be married to God and me too!"

It was a bright day early in the spring of 1977 and the place was at the base of Colt Run Holler in Roane County, West Virginia. Jack was all stirred up and he had no intentions of departing the premises without an explanation. I had tried to clarify my situation but the word celibacy and the concept were not in his vocabulary or imagination, just as my speedy exodus from a fast city life to solitude in the mountains was a mystery to most people I knew. I yearned to listen for the still small Voice in an atmosphere of pristine wilderness. After four and a half years of working in the inner city neighborhoods of Chicago my whole being ached for a life of silence, simplicity and prayer on the fringe of society, and yet one close enough to folks to be able to go out from time to time to do service.

Since arriving on wild and wonderful West Virginia soil six months earlier, Jack had so generously taught me some essential homesteading skills and helped with direly needed maintenance on the abandoned house I now called home. In those early days he occasionally rode his "Ford," (an aged riding lawn mower with a small wagon hitched at the rear), down into the holler to help with cutting grass. In his fifties, he had hinted more than once during those occasions that his search for a good woman was still on and... I would fit the bill.

The front door was scarcely ever locked but one particular evening I had spied him trailing me down the hill after I had spent a long day of work out in the town. A gutsy feeling was crawling across my inners that he was experiencing deep loneliness and looking for a mate more than ever. The intuition was right. Only after passionate, prolonged entreaties on his part to be let in and polite but firm refusals on my part to open the door did Jack finally leave the porch and wind his way out of the holler and go back up to his home on Colt Ridge Road. He was my initial, authentic introduction to West Virginia's rural mountain culture.

Before Spencer was Spencer, our town was called Tanner's Crossroads. Those earliest settlers to Roane County spent the first winter here under a rock cave ledge on the sight of the present day Spencer Middle School. Jack came from sturdy stock. For awhile he worked up in Akron, Ohio in a factory because jobs were so scarce here but, like many a native West Virginia man of his time he found laboring away from the country and the hills just too foreign so he came home. One day he told me: "I took care of mom and dad before they died here in this very house."

Jack could not read nor write so that limited his opportunities for a job. As he aged he developed poor circulation in his lower extremities and could not be on his feet for long periods of time or they would turn a mottled purple. He was able to get some government assistance. Usually he kept occupied fixing some farm equipment or gardening or gathering in wood for the winter. Whenever he was able, he could be found helping his neighbors with whatever needed "fixin."

This son of the mountains loved to chat with folks and especially while planted in the swing on his front porch. Sometimes he admitted to them: "I get awful lonely for a woman." One day when I came to his abode Jack showed me the kitchen of his little house and I remarked that the sink was positioned very low, only about thirty inched from the ground. He quipped: "That is for a short woman." I remember saying to myself:

"No radical feminist would ever abide this place!" - Not that I was one of those, but if I was meant to be in the married state I wouldn't want to be dubbed my husband's "ole lady and servant."

Above the sink was a small window that overlooked the downward-sloping backyard and the wooded hills in the distance. He said: "This is where I hunt in deer season," - claiming that "Yes," in fact he did fell bucks from that vantage point.

A retired refrigerator served as his cabinet for plates, cups, plastic margarine bowls and silverware. If a person came to his place for something to eat, they could have a spoon or a fork, but not both. No chairs were in the tiny kitchen. Jack usually ate on the couch or seated in the old recliner near the wood stove. Guests got the sofa. The heating stove was a huge old, rust colored, metal barrel drum perched on cement blocks with a door forged into the front of it for loading wood. A pipe was welded to the top of it that extended out through the ceiling and roof. In the summer Jack put a bucket over the opening of the pipe up there to keep out the rain. He was never cold in the winter. In fact he often had to open the front door of the house to be able to breathe.

His plumbing apparatus was one notch up the scale from mine. He had a cistern well which caught rain water off the tin roof, proceeded down a drain spout through a metal, fifty-five gallon drum with pebbles for filtration, and then into a cement well. He rigged it to a pump, which fed the water into the kitchen sink and bathroom. From the bathroom the water and sewage went into a black pipe and down the hill in the back to the outhouse. Once the health department heard of this unique setup and a representative came to visit telling him that he needed an approved septic system, to which Jack replied: "You pay for it and I'll get it in." Jack told me: "I never heard from them no more."

The next time I saw him he said to me: "Give me a poke and I'll give you some apples."

"A what?" I asked. He replied:

"You know, a poke, a brown paper sack." So began my first lesson in some local expressions. Another day it was: "Jeanne you're fallin off!"

"I'm what?" I replied with a big question mark in my eyes.

"You are losing weight."

On a wintery afternoon he told me he got a new to-boggan and I was looking around for a sled. Here it was the knitted cap perched on the top of his head.

One time he sighed and remarked: "I sure wish I could get shed of this cold!"

"Get shed?" I asked.

"Yes, get rid of this cold. It's hangin' on forever." Learning these and so many more sayings were part of enculturation to this West Virginia County.

Another aspect to life in the hills here is trading. On the local radio station, WVRC, there is a program called; The Trading Post in which folks can call in and state what they want to buy, sell, or trade. Jack was on it every day trading one thing or another; a knife for a rifle, a pump for a mower, and a chain saw for a dog. Just name it. He even traded for a car and he could not drive.

One day he got on the air and I heard him invite everybody and anybody that might want to come to join in his birthday party. I really had to give him credit. He took steps so that he would not be lonely for the celebration and he ordered enough sheet cake and ice cream to easily feed thirty people. A few of us did show up and so he had the Happy Birthday. Lots of cake and ice cream went to his freezer for good times later on.

One Christmas he invited some local people for Christmas dinner and I said to him: "Jack, what are you going to have?"

"I was thinking of hamburgers and orange soda pop. " He replied. My stomach did a rapid flip at the thought and I offered to bring some fried chicken, mashed potatoes and cranberries. His response was all in the affirmative. He did not care a fig for what there was to eat, just so there were folks to share it with.

Jack did not have much "book learnin," as he called it but he had knowledge that many folks never attain plus a deep sensitivity to life and the created world around him. He knew practically every plant and local tree by name and could tell you the uses for most of them. He grew the very best garden veggies and fruits. Sometimes that was with a little assist from Miracle Grow and a lot of tender loving care. He showed me where he had thrown some peach pits a few years back and in that place stood two trees which were simply laden with fresh peaches.

On one of the occasions when he came down with his mower to help me get rid of the "jungle" surrounding my little shack he accidentally caught a piece of barbed wire in the whirring blade of his old riding lawnmower and the wire swung around gouging him in the leg. Because I am a nurse, I was really worried that he would come down with tetanus. He never had a tetanus shot so I went to the local hospital to get him one. I was on my way out Colt Ridge Road to give it to him and he got someone to drive him in the OPPOSITE direction. No way was he going to take an injection. He said: I'll smear pine tar over it and it will be just fine." It took a lot of teaching about lockjaw and the consequences before he allowed me to administer it to him. Even then I believe the only reason he acquiesced was to placate me.

Never one to be concerned about appearances or health needs Jack was toothless and gummed whatever he ate. Finally after much persuasion he went to a dentist to see about getting a pair of dentures so that he would be able to eat more of a variety of foods. Well…he must have gone for the cheapest set. He went from being toothless to having a mouth filled with the biggest, whitest, widest, horse teeth a person has ever seen! When Jack flashed that first smile with those new dentures it was so hard to keep from bending over double with laughter. He looked much better without the teeth! Of course no one wanted to hurt his feelings but it was hard to keep from splitting your sides at his altered facial expression.

Although Jack had little formal education or religious formation he had a deep spiritual sensitivity and he believed in a God or Father Who loved him and made all the beauties of creation. He did keep getting Jesus mixed up with Moses. Despite a lack of intellectual input Jack possessed an intuitive dimension and wisdom about life. He told me once he had a sister named Jessie, who was sick for a long time before she passed on. One day when we were in the woods we came across a thicket and he said: "I saw my sister here when she passed away." I said:

"Jack, what do you mean?" He replied:

I was walking through here one day and she was there in that thicket. I saw her face. Later in the day when I got home Mom said to me: "Jack, I have some bad news for you." I said:

"I know what it is. Jessie died. She appeared before me down in the woods."

Another time a local doctor recommended that Jack have a "herny repair" as he called it, nothing serious.

Before friends knew it, Jack was making out a will. This one gets the house and land. Sister Jane gets the little golden goose with the small change in it. I was to get his wooden hutch, and another was bequeathed his shotgun. He even signed away his precious wheelbarrow that he used for everything from toting wood to hauling various and sundry items all over the little plot of land he owned. Of course there was no real money to dispose of.

Then came the day when he needed a ride to the hospital and asked if I would take him. One of his sisters, Emma, came to say: "Goodbye Jack. I'll see you when you get back." He turned to her and said: "Emma, I'm not coming back."

Off we went on an hour and a half drive to St. Joseph's Hospital in Parkersburg. When we got there his face was flushed. I knew he was upset. Jack and hospitals were just not compatible. The surroundings were so unfamiliar. When his blood pressure was taken it was escalating. I guess the medical personnel got it down with antihypertensive drugs because the next morning he went for the surgery. All seemed to go well during the operation but afterwards it seemed everything that could go wrong, did. Two days later when a couple of us went to visit him, his abdomen was horribly distended. Tubes were coming from nearly every orifice. He tried to speak to us through his oxygen mask asking: "How are the donkeys doing?" And…he wanted to know if he could have a kiss.

Jack did not make it and he knew he was not going to. Till this day I do not understand what happened after surgery and I was not family so pertinent information was not given to me. What was supposed to have been a minor procedure left him with complications that were critical and then turned abruptly – terminal. The best modern medicine had to offer was not good enough.

A little cortege of family and friends followed the casket to Mount Olive Cemetery. Up it wound among the cedars to a hilltop overlooking a meadow dappled with gold flowers. White blossoming dogwoods dotted the landscape and the red bud trees with their lacy fuchsia foliage greeted our procession. Cattle grazed contentedly in nearby pastures. The azure blue sky was laced with birdsong that seemed to sing: "Come on Home Jack."

With his passing it seemed to me an era had ended. Winding our way back down the mountainside I reflected on my own origin on the planet and how I found myself falling in love with this Appalachian land and her people.

CHAPTER **2**

Father – the Real Meaning

Search (Wisdom) out, discover her; seek her and you will find her. (Sirach 6:28)

In high school my classmates were taken up with all the normal things: the current fashions, Rock n' Roll, jitterbugging, and boys. I felt so odd and out of place because my interests did not lie with theirs and I could not even force myself to be in search of the same things. Sometimes there was an awful loneliness. It would have been wonderful to be popular, to get caught up in their excitement, but the innate attraction to like what they were treasuring eluded me. I experienced a gnawing emptiness at a gut level and I knew "things" or any one person couldn't fill the void. I was yearning to be caught up, free, in love with life, real life, with a sense of deep purpose and direction. My musings were more on the future; what it held, how I could find true joy and the way to discover Who God was, what He was like, and what His desires were for my life.

The lifestyle at home was frugal, although we never went hungry. Mom never bought a new dress or any food as expensive as a beef roast. We always went for that to

Sunday dinner at my single aunts' and uncle's house. They had the prime beef. At home there were dishes of fried, broiled, stewed, roasted and baked chicken, along with hens' eggs — poached, boiled, fried, scrambled and over easy. Our clothes were expertly sewn from gaily printed chicken feed bags and what other material could be found on sale by mom. We kept heat and lights to the bare minimum. We scarcely ever went anywhere and never out to eat.

All the time, unbeknownst to us, dad was amassing wealth in mutual funds, stocks and bonds. Nearly every penny was banked, pocketed or invested. Even when I made seventy-five cents an hour baby – sitting Dad demanded much of that. None of us kids got allowances. My Aunt Gert paid my Catholic High School tuition and my younger siblings went to public schools. College for me was out of the question. Dad's responses to my requests were invariably: "No."

As I look back now, it seems that the horrors of the Great Depression affected folks in basically two ways; either it left them sharing the little they had with others in need and then hoping for the best to happen, or it left folks with a tenacious, gut wrenching fear that the horrible crunch of material impoverishment might occur again. The resolution therefore was; amass as much wealth as possible to fend off any repetition of the same state of affairs. Dad appeared to be the second type. The end result was that it left him grasping and anxious about the morrow.

His hours of labor were long and intensive without much time for play or interaction with his family. He would rise early to feed the thousands of chickens inhabiting our three story chicken barn and collect all those eggs. Besides running the poultry farm, he erected our buff brick home with the help of our maternal granddad, (a retired carpenter,) by salvaging any useable lumber from wrecked homes. He helped and taught his family how to plant and manage a huge vegetable garden with enough veggies to feed ourselves and take out, along with the poultry and eggs we had readied, to sell to others. There was a time, when in addition to all this he worked a part-time job at Homestead Valve Factory. One night coming home from the plant a little later than usual he jumped over a wall and landed in an uncovered pit, injuring his back and fracturing a couple of vertebrae. From then on any heavy labor was painful for him. How mom prayed dad would find work as she became employed at the new Pittsburgh International Airport flower shop! The prayers were answered when my great-aunt, Sister Rose Vincent SC, a teacher, put in a good word for him with one of her former students in city government. Dad was permitted to take a civil service math test - a preliminary to becoming a tax assessor. He scored at the top and got the job.

One day my father squinted his eyes, screwed up his nose and said to me in utter seriousness: "Money counts." Inside my head I heard:

"And nothing else does: Right dad? Not feelings, or friends or playfulness, or service, or generosity…"

On another occasion, when it was chilly outside, I was sitting at the table in the kitchen when he came up behind me and whacked me across the back, shouting: "I told you not to leave the bedroom window open!" When he learned that I was not the one who did it there was no word of apology.

Fear took hold of me…as it had him, only in different arenas.

Every time I would try to strike up a serious conversation with Dad the words would lock in my throat. I remember one evening when I was about sixteen. I stood in the hallway, just around the corner from the kitchen where he stood by the sink. I so longed to talk over with him some of my deepest desires for the future and I could not push myself into the room. Tears welled up from some deep cavern within and I went to my room in silence, choking back wracking sobs with the realization that I could not communicate with my own father.

He would compare me with others and wonder why I did not bring home grades, all A's like some of my classmates. He could not understand why I did not have the same desires in life that he did. I never heard a word of affirmation or encouragement.

Once I asked him what he would like to see me become and the answer was; "a legal secretary or an airline hostess." I asked:

"Why would you want me in those jobs dad?" He replied:

"So I'd be able to get free air miles and good legal advice."

I spent many solitary moments quietly before God among the thickets in the woods down behind our home. Hours were spent silently in the high school chapel trying to hear, to fathom what I was called to believe and do. It was a horrific inner struggle with no outer guidance. Was it even possible to discern and take the right path? Was Jesus and His Good News for real? If He was, He demanded a response.

What happened then has ever been counted as sheer grace. There is a book entitled: *The Perfect Joy of St. Francis* by Felix Timmerman. To this day I cannot remember how it fell into my hands. Once I began perusing the piece it was impossible to put it down. My heart throbbed with excitement. It was an "aha" moment for me, even though St. Francis or Il Poverello (The little poor one,) as he was dubbed by the town folk of his day, was born in Assisi, Italy in 1181. He was the son of a rich cloth merchant, Pietro Bernadone, one of the upper crust, in a rising middle class. His father was thoroughly intent on becoming as rich as he could be. Pietro traveled far and wide to bring back the most expensive cloths to his shop. One day a beggar entered the store and asked for alms for the love of God. Pietro scorned him. Francis, who was helping out in the store at the time, refused him too. Later, thinking better of it, Francis went after the beggar, asked forgiveness, and took care of him.

Another incident is one in which Francis came upon a leper with stinking sores and rotting flesh. His first response was that of absolute horror and total revulsion. However, Francis forced himself to go and kiss the leper and give him alms. The story has it that when he rode on and looked back the leper was nowhere in sight. Francis was given to understand that the leper was Christ, Himself. Later on Francis speaking of that moment, would say: "What was bitter was turned into sweetness."

He had seen firsthand how the love of money was snaring his father's soul and tethering it tight with greed. He had experienced in the embrace of the leper a mystical moment of transforming joy.

In his youth, Francis was a spendthrift, who threw lavish

parties and wore the finest clothes, (made of course from his father's luxurious materials). He was a singing minstrel and troubadour type of the Middle Ages, generous and loved by almost everyone. He had a chivalrous heart and wanted to be a knight. However, one day clad in an expensive suit of shining armor and riding off to conquer a foreign land he heard a voice. "Francis, who is it better to serve the master or the servant?"

"Why the master," Francis replied. The voice came again:

"Why are you serving the servant?" Francis was overcome. He turned his mount and headed home. He went off to a deserted place and spent a lot of time in a cave in prayer pondering the meaning of the words he had heard and what was being asked of him.

Once he changed clothes with an astonished pauper of the streets just to get the feel of doing something hard for the love of God. Another time he went around the town as a beggar, to the deep consternation of his father who found him, beat him up and imprisoned him in a dungeon so he would come back to his senses.

Francis finally came to realize that his deep inner call was to become totally divested of earthly riches so he could serve the Master freely. In his poverty he was paradoxically filled with a joy the world has seldom seen. He changed his sumptuous robes permanently to don a poor, patched brownish–gray tunic and a cord. He went unshod to work with the lepers and to rebuild churches. He preached with a fiery passion about the love of God and the need for penance. Not long after his own conversion thousands of men from all walks of life came to follow him. His first followers were known as the Order of Friars Minor.

Shortly after I had finished reading the book and was wondering how to imbibe some of that spirit in my own life, our yearly high school retreat began. (A retreat then was a week set apart within the high school curriculum for extra prayer, reflection and listening to conferences on spiritual themes). What a surprise it was to see a Friar Minor, one of St. Francis' modern day sons, up there in front of us giving the conferences! He was in his late twenties, rather gaunt, bearded, garbed in a brown tunic type affair with a capuche (hood), a rope around his waist, and sandals on his feet. He was almost dancing off the altar steps in his glee and zest for life. He was a ragamuffin bursting with joy and eager to help others find what he had.

With vocation questions rolling around in my head I approached this spiritual son of Francis. His name was Father Angelus Shaughnessy.

"Do you suppose I could talk with you?" I said. His head nodded in the affirmative so I nervously and gingerly began the conversation. In a few moments I had spurted out the thoughts of my heart and the dreams that were percolating in my brain, book-ending it all by saying: "I think I might like to be a Franciscan." A gracious smile crossed his face, just as if another fish was caught for Christ.

Not long after that encounter I joined and made profession in what was known in those days as the Third Order of St. Francis. It was the branch of the Order founded by Francis for those who lived out in society and not behind monastic or convent walls. I was elected as head (or prefect,) of our high school fraternity. Every month it was necessary to go to Pittsburgh to join the other professed, high school prefects at the monastery for teaching sessions. There, I wore out the doorsteps of the wise man and listened to Father Angelus' discerning mind. I found a "father "to lead and gently guide. He was the one Providence sent to direct my footsteps on a path that would become a labyrinth of comings and goings until I finally found the spot where roots could grow deep.

With Father Angelus I could open my heart and spill the inners out without fear of reprisal, anger or diminishment. He would listen intently, gently correct and lead, humble and encourage with the infinite finesse of one who loves much. I only needed a few of his sentences to guide me, such as: "You are on the right track. Follow that inner prompting soon. It is God inside you. Don't hold anything back. Give all. Don't be afraid. Your father will <u>not</u> have a nervous breakdown as he says he will."

Father Angelus buoyed up my hope and self confidence and set my feet on a path diametrically opposed to my dad's view of a good life, but in total resonance with the dream in my mind and in sync with the heartbeats in my chest.

CHAPTER 3

Behind the Walls

I love them that love me; and those that seek me early shall find me. (Proverbs: 8: 17)

The motherhouse of the Sisters of St. Francis of the Providence of God rested peacefully on a hillside in the South Hills area of Pittsburgh. Father Angelus loved that community and highly recommended that I inquire about admission. Soon after high school graduation, I was on the "Mount," as we called it, studying the scene. A huge edifice of dark brick was the convent. Two deeply colored red doors marked the entranceway. A newly erected chapel was attached to the convent. A huge statue of Saint Michael the Archangel towered above the front doors; standing like a sentry on the mountain. Other structures on the premises were a high school, where the sisters taught, a prep building housing younger aspirants to the sisterhood and a few other smaller buildings, one of which was home to the community chaplain, Father Joe.

The red doors swung open to sixteen of us on September 8, 1959. The mistress of the novitiate, and the one mainly responsible for our formation in religious life, ushered her new charges over the threshold. Most of us were in our late teens and we entered into staid living room parlors with ornamental rugs, high backed stuffed chairs and cabinets lined with Lithuanian memorabilia. I had not read about anything as grand as this in The Perfect Joy of St. Francis, but if this was what it took to become a Franciscan I was more than willing to give it my best efforts.

We donned long black dresses; the attire of the neophytes of the community. We were known as Postulants. We had to pull on gross, opaque, lengthy black stockings and the most repulsive looking, shiny, black, lace up granny shoes with three inch cube heels. I had seen them only on aged, hunched backed Italian women in our parish church at funeral times. Added to the dress was a black cape with a white collar. Crowning all that was a transparent blackish veil extending down over the shoulders. We were allowed family pictures in those outfits, with our loved ones, beneath the shade of the white pompon bushes outside the parlor doors. With tearful farewells, we took our leave and were whisked away behind the solid, heavy walls of our convent home.

Then we were introduced to the new surroundings. One wing of the huge building was reserved for the fully professed sisters. The other wing comprised the novitiate premises, where those in training to be religious sisters lived. The postulant dormitory was on the third floor. In it were sixteen metal beds covered by white spreads and each bed was surrounded by an overhead railing from which were suspended white privacy curtains. When the curtains were pulled around the bed, it comprised what is known as a "cell." Tiny hospital-like stands were situated by each bed and contained the necessaries for daily living; more black stockings, tee - shirts, underwear, handkerchiefs, toi-letries etc. There was one straight backed wooden chair apiece. A big crucifix was the only ornamentation on the walls and it happened to be in my space: an omen of things to come.

On the first floor was the novitiate community room. All the postulants and novices and first professed sisters gathered here, mostly for studying religious texts, college assignments, and for recreation. Most of the time recre-ation revolved around talking about our days and darning holes in those black stockings or tee - shirts. Sometimes in the winter we experienced gleeful escapades of toboggan-ing over the hills in the newly fallen snow.

When the postulant year was nearly finished and, if we were accepted as novices in the community, we had to submit three names, one of which we would like to be called in religious life. That did not mean we would get one of the three, only that they were our preferences. Naturally, a name that already existed was off limits. Choices such as Francis and Clare were out of the question. I chose Janine, Michelle, or Patrick but wasn't that much attached to what I was named.

During the year preceding becoming a novice there was a book being read in the refectory (dining room,) dur-ing our meals that totally captured my attention. It was entitled: Walled in Light, by Mother Mary Francis PCC. It was a biography of St. Colette of Corbie. She was baptized Nicolette, and was the only offspring of an aged couple. Colette lived as an anchoress (a person consecrated to God and walled up in a tiny enclosure usually attached to the parish church). Her life was to be one of prayer and simple manual labor. After several years she was called by God to reform the Order of Poor Clares (the second order that St. Francis founded along with Saint Clare). I became absolutely enthralled with the life of St. Colette. She spent so much time in contemplation and then Christ used her so powerfully, yet gently, to bring back the Poor Clare Sisters to the first or primitive observance of the rule as St. Clare had lived it.

I was feeling the need for more time for prayer, quiet reflection, and closer ties to St. Francis' Lady Poverty and less time for study. I did not know what to do. And so the days went on until we were to receive the religious habit, and the white veil of the novice along with our new name. We all processed in a straight line down the center aisle of the chapel in our white wedding dresses, to the sung refrain: "Come spouse of Christ..." We went behind the main altar into the sacristy (the room usually behind the sanctuary or altar of the church,) and exchanged our bridal finery for the garb of the community and came out to kneel at the altar rail and receive our new names: "Mary Ann, you shall be called Sister Alexis. Elizabeth your name will be Sister Margaret. Rebecca, your name will be Sister Vianney." At last came my turn: "Jeanne, in religious life you shall be called Sister Nicolette." I turned white and nearly fell off the altar step, totally taken aback by the pronouncement. Somewhere in the deep cavernous hole of my heart I knew this would have a profound meaning in my life. Receiving her as my patron was not just a mere coincidence. Time would reveal the deeper intimations.

In the novice year getting dressed was more of a challenge as was the life. We had fifteen minutes to get our garb on in the right order and then be in the chapel for morning prayer. First, the black habit made of serge with multiple pleats front and back and wide belled like sleeves was pulled over our heads. After the habit we donned the crucifix, the cord with three knots symbolizing the three vows of poverty, chastity and obedience that we would make as professed sisters. Following in succession, we put on the coif made of white linen which encircled the face and was pinned to tailor fit the back of the head with tiny safety pins. It had to be taut or in a few minutes the strands of hair would come sprawling out over the temples and down across our foreheads. The guimpe was next. It was made of white celluloid and brittle. This piece covered the chest and was tied behind the neck with a string. The last item was the veil and it covered the head and extended down our backs. It was pinned to the coif with little ball headed white straight pins.

If a novice, in that wee hour of the morning, should accidently forget to put on the crucifix, the guimpe and all the head apparel would have to be taken off and then replaced. Added to this, there were prayers to be said as each article of clothing was put on. Then there would be no chance of making it to the chapel on time. Repercussions would follow. Novices were forever getting "penances" or acts of mortification to atone for "faults" from the Mistress of the novitiate. I used to think the United States Marines had nothing on us.

We sat for meditation three to a pew, one novice on each end and one in the middle. One morning Sister Patrick, the middle one, had gotten her habit on back-wards and I watched out of the side of my eye, stifling giggles as she attempted to turn the whole thing around in the chapel without attracting the attention of the mistress. No luck. She had to pray a long time with outstretched arms for that faux pas.

During our novice year we had more time for silence and prayer, theological and religious studies, formation and reflection. A churning storm was brewing inside me because I was being primed to be a teacher in a school of the order. There were no long periods of quiet prayer that I had read about in the life of St. Francis. I was not going to be living with the poor or with any modern day "lepers." It was true we did not have much in the way of any personal possessions but everything we needed was provided. There was talk of a new wing being built onto the motherhouse which would contain private bedrooms and a swimming pool. I deeply loved my sisters in training with me. They were wonderful women but I was not a peace. Where was the "Perfect Joy?"

"What is wrong with me?" I would ask over and over. "Why can't I just be content and happy?"

"O God what do I do? Where do I go? Don't let me make vows here if I cannot keep them!"

I was writing out invitations for my first profession of vows when I literally could no longer make the pen move. Retrieving the invites I had written I went and stood trembling before the door of our mistress' office, Sister Germaine. A sister was in the room speaking with her. When she came out, I could not step over the threshold. It was then, with one swift push from Sister Patrick, standing behind me (and also waiting to see the mistress), I landed in the middle of her office and stammered: "I have to go." Sister Germaine replied:

"You are in an agony aren't you?"

"Yes." I nodded my head. She said to me:

"If you cannot accept poverty the way we profess it here you cannot stay on in the community. What do you think you will do now?"

"I will go and talk to Father Angelus and see about joining the Poor Clares." I had heard they had a monastery in Cleveland.

Sister Germaine called my parents. I had to go up to the dormitory while the others were at noonday prayer, change back into civilian clothes, and be whisked away without so much as one word of farewell to those whose friendship I cherished. Yes, it was an agony, and back home in a familiar bed that night I slept not a wink.

Father Angelus was surprised to hear my voice and even more surprised to find out that I had left the Mount. I told him I would like to make an application to join the Poor Clares. I felt very much drawn to longer periods of quiet prayer and a life of more poverty. He was okay with that but I could sense that he was not one hundred percent in agreement with my choice. He felt uneasy. At any rate, a few months later I was admitted as a postulant at the Poor Clare Colettines in Cleveland. I did not know at the time that this was an enclosed monastery belonging to the reform movement of St. Colette. It was a community where the sisters rarely went out for anything except, medical emergencies. They wore no shoes, donned rough wool habits, got up in the middle of the night to pray, and chanted the Divine Office of the church (which consisted mostly of psalms,) many times a day. There was daily Mass and meditation. We had no secular studies, but only religious instruction, formation and some theological treatises and conferences. We cooked, cleaned, gardened and made altar breads. The life was far more ascetic and quiet but living with the Poor Clares I was not at "home." The life did not fit like a hand in a glove. Our Mother Abbess (the superior,) would speak from time to time about the poor on the other side of the city. I wondered to myself: "Do I belong among those folks; the poor? Am I being tempted by the devil to leave religious life?" One day, as a novice, I screamed at God: "Lord, if You do not want me here get me out!"

One week later I was summoned into the mistress' office and Sister Amata Rose floored me with the words: "You have to go. Holy Mother St. Colette loves you very much but, this is not your place."

Dazed as I was at the pronouncement, I felt some relief and realized in her words that the will of God was being made manifest. - Not that I had a clue as to what the next step would be or when God would ever speak to my heart again.

Back home once more I was near despair. I did not fit the structures. I could not see. Willy-nilly, I crossed the wise man's threshold once more. Father Angelus probably thought: Now what? Just what was I to say? All was so nebulous except that I still yearned for a life of deep contemplative prayer, to be poor among the poor, and to vow a life of celibacy within the Franciscan family.

Father Angelus showed me a way. He received me back into the Secular Franciscan Order I had joined in high school and accepted my private vows of poverty, chastity and obedience under the framework of that Order's Rule.

Much to the chagrin of my parents I left home and went to live alone in a ghetto area of Pittsburgh, which was not far from the friar's monastery or from the location where our group of lay Franciscans had their monthly meetings. Here, I found the time my soul needed to be prayerful and quiet before God. It was easy to almost get lost in the silence of the huge church. The poor and indigent were in close proximity to my little apartment, so I worked among the families and especially with the children. They taught me much about life.

Dad put in a good word for me at a temporary agency and I got hired as a clerk for a steel company where, filing, stuffing envelopes and later, typing invoices allowed me to save up enough funds to become a nurse.

One day in the early seventies, after repeated, urgent pleas to God to help me find some Franciscan community to share more deeply with, I opened a magazine in the little kitchen of an apartment on Mintwood Street. My heart started to pound. I sensed an awakening. The piece was entitled: In Pursuit of the Charism at Armitage St. in Chicago. It told of a group of Franciscans: friars, sisters and lay folks who lived and worked right among the poor Hispanics and Blacks on the streets of the "windy city." They took part-time jobs so that there would be extra time for prayer and outreach. They lived separately in the same building but came together for some meals and daily prayer. The group was called the "Gospel Family." I sensed: "This is it." However, the magazine article listed no one to write to or get in touch with. What to do?!

A few days after reading the article I went to Communion one day at Mass and heard a voice inside me say: "Go talk to Fr. Gus." Was I hearing things? Fr. Augustine Milon ofm, who everyone called Fr. Gus, headed up a charismatic prayer group that I attended on Wednesdays. It was in McKees Rocks, not far from Pittsburgh.

The following week, feeling awkward, I approached him after the meeting and asked if he had ever heard of the Gospel Family in Chicago. To my utter amazement he replied: "The friars there are my community and I have the address and phone number." God's timing! I had just finished my nurse's training. In a couple months, and after a few phone calls to the "family," Sister Miriam Friday contacted me and said: "Come on!"

Within a few days, on September 14, 1972, a Greyhound bus, bound for the huge city of Chicago, carried at least one passenger up and over Skyline Drive closer to her destiny.

CHAPTER 4

Life in the Windy City

After all there is but one race-humanity. (Bending of the Bough, III by George Moore)

The bus spiraled down into a dark underground tunnel, and came to a halt. As I descended the Greyhound steps and entered the Chicago main terminal a flood of underground lights, the odor of human sweat, and the earthy smells of a sea of bustling humanity enveloped me. Brother Dominic Figura and Kristine Pierie, of the "Gospel Family," stepped out of that throng of people to receive me with huge smiles, open hearts and limping gaits. Dominic, a Franciscan brother in his late fifties, had suffered from polio in his youth and youthful Kris was born with spina bifida which eventually caused her to lose her lower left leg. She wore a prosthesis. After hugs of a cheery warm welcome and an attempt to retrieve my suitcase, (which did not make it on the same trip,) we went out to the community van. The machine – of an ugly, nondescript, gray hue was so rickety it seemed it would go bust at any provocation. The vehicle reeked with the scents of decaying vegetables and fruits.

I soon learned that the stench in the van was due to the frequent trips to the open markets and dumps, where some of the "family" members would garner and beg food for the poor of the city and then haul around all the produce to where folks were in need. Dominic knew all the back alleys and where to collect "treasures" like newspapers and cans which were then redeemed for money to keep the contraption rolling.

We drove up to 1024 W. Armitage St. on the near north side of the city and I spied a building with a flying buttress, (a black ornate architectural outcropping on the corner of the structure), with peeling paint and some of its rattling window corners stuffed with cardboard. The first floor, loaded with junk and debris, was locked. The Franciscan Sisters and lay women dwelt on the second floor while the friars and the lay men lived on the third. The fourth floor housed the owners: two black guys, and above them was their penthouse on the roof, replete with turf and plants! It overlooked the Black, Puerto Rican and American Indian enclaves on the bustling, littered streets below.

A narrow, decrepit, staircase led up to the women's apartment. Once inside, everything was clean and tidy even though all the furniture was second hand and nothing matched. We had a section of a sectional sofa, some lumpy stuffed chairs, a two - cushioned, dilapidated couch and a threadbare rug. The dining area contained a long rectangular table and a host of mismatched, straight back chairs. Individuals off the streets often came and sat themselves down in them to share a meal with the community. The kitchen and bathroom linoleums sported jagged, random holes. The building had seen its heyday in the 1940's and had gone downhill since then. Sister Miriam, Sister

Madge, Kris and I shared those rooms and upstairs were the Franciscan Friars: Fathers Sergius, Blase, Jerry and Brother Dominic. Keith Fisher, Al DeGarie and Albert Nix completed the resident group.

During the first night in the city I cringed and contracted in bed every time the sonic sound of the elevated train came barreling past the window. I heard a gun blast rip through the air at 11:00 pm. The next day I was told one of the Little Sisters of Jesus on the south side of the city was recently slain when a stray bullet entered her room at night thru the window, ricocheted off the wall, and killed her. "O God did I make the right choice in coming here?!" That was the phrase that rolled around in my brain for a couple of days. Eventually the fear subsided and the loving individuals surrounding me buoyed up my hope and resolve.

A lot of ferment and fomentation was taking place in our church and in society. The whole attempt at renewal promoted by Vatican Council II instructed religious orders to return to the spirit of their founding fathers or mothers. They responded by leaving behind many of the big institutions and going back out into the fray, out among the poor where things were not safe or tidy but messy and sometimes extremely dangerous. Most nuns left their religious garb, classrooms, hospitals and oftentimes religious life itself. In civil society we witnessed dramatic opposition to the Vietnam War by the SDS (Students for a Democratic Society). Some of those drafted into the military service became conscientious objectors and were ostracized by their families. Some people chose to join the Catholic Worker Movement and the founder, Dorothy Day, who lived and proclaimed pacifist principals. They refused to pay the telephone tax that supported the war effort. Our Gospel Family was comprised of or connected with it all.

In 1969 when the friars heard the call of Vatican Council II to return to the spirit of St. Francis, they followed a call to live a poor lifestyle with the poor. Fr. Sergius Wroblewski ofm, from the Pulaski Province of the Order of Friars Minor, was looking for some others to join him Fr. Blasé Karas, Brother Dominic Figura and Br. Tom LaPointe signed on, leaving behind them the monastery walls and the quiet life. Kathy and Phil Dahl-Bredine, a young couple belonging to the Catholic Worker group had a place of hospitality in the city and they invited the friars to live in their building. The Dahl-Bredines assisted the friars in the huge transition from monastic routine to life in the inner city among the people. Father Sergius was a teacher and a dynamic preacher: It was not long before two of his hearers, both Franciscan Sisters, wanted to be involved in the new way of life. After that some lay folks joined who were political activists, war resisters, or who like I, wanted to be more identified with and in close proximity to the poor of society. We formed what was called an intentional community in that we were united for a specific purpose; to live the Gospel life in the spirit of St. Francis of Assisi.

Immersed in these surroundings, I soon felt more at home and much closer to what I had read about in *The Perfect Joy of St. Francis*. Needy, poor, and hurting folks brushed shoulders with us every day; on the streets, at our doorways, and around our table. St Francis' spirit and the lifestyle he embraced were lived out experientially by the brothers and sisters and my heart was much more at peace. I did not know if this way of life was to be my permanent one but, for the "now" I believed this is where I was meant to be.

We all had part-time work for self support. This provision enabled us to have more time to spend in prayer and in one on one contact in our relationships with the folks around us. Brothers Dominic and Tom were engaged in St. Joseph's Work co-op where they used their carpentry skills to refurbish abandoned and ransacked apartments to make places available for low income folks. The priests were away most weekends taking care of parish ministries or preaching. During the rest of the week they were present to the needs of the neighborhood and the folks who came to the door. Some of the rest of us did cleaning jobs, or daycare work, or ran a storefront half a block away where folks could buy second hand clothes for a quarter or gather round a table for a cup of coffee and camaraderie. I did some part-time nursing at a nearby hospital and later in a clinic that serviced thousands of the city's poor. Some of us went out on day-labor work to get a good idea of what it was like to share the fate of the misplaced and homeless. I did that once. A bunch of us were treated more like numbers than individuals. Herded into buses from a central location, factory owners had us whisked away to their plants on the outskirts of the city. Once at the worksite we were in with the ex-cons, the newly arrived Asians, the Blacks and Hispanics and all manner of people who had no other job source. The overseers kept us on our feet all day except for a brief bag lunch period. We scarcely ever had a bathroom break. One day I was packaging Grecian Formula 16 for men and my location was at the end of the assembly line. I noticed the manager eyeing me (maybe because he thought I had more concentration than some of the others), and before long he motioned that I go to the front of the line where the job was to cork the bottles as they came swiftly down the conveyor belt and then slam the cork head down with a hammer. It was nerve wracking. By the end of the day I wreaked of the "formula." At the table that evening the community wondered who was emitting the strange odor. Father Jerry who had gone to a workplace then, was no less fortunate. He was sent to a packaging and stacking place and the foreman shouted at him: "I've seen stupid people in my life but you take the cake!"

The men's apartment didn't smell quite as good as ours and cleanliness was not their top priority so for obvious reasons and, by consensus, the chapel was on the women's floor. We met daily in it for morning and evening prayer. On most days the community went to Mass at the little parish Church of St. Teresa's across the street.

We all came together for the evening meal. Each resident member had to take their turn at fixing it. Some of us had specialties and Sergius had one specialty and he was really good at it: cream of tomato soup with chunks of beef in it. We all knew if he was cooking what was going to be on the menu. One day when it was Blasé's turn to cook he pulled a package out of the freezer that had been given him by Luv. She was an elderly woman who spent much of her time on the city streets. This gift was her contribution, "out of love," for the community meal. Blase took the package and left it in the refrigerator to thaw. What a surprise, when, after a busy day he went to cook it for supper. Indeed, it had been a huge fish. Now it had a head and a tail and nothing in the middle! Peanut butter was the main entrée that night as it was sometimes on other evenings when the cook expected eight for supper and thirteen showed up. Guests were served first and they were the hungriest of all. What a difference from convent life where all the loaded dishes rolled in on carts, where it was known exactly how many mouths were to be fed. This experience was much more like what I had read about in *The Perfect Joy*…

On Wednesday evenings we gathered for Mass, a meal, and a talk, usually given by our leader, Fr. Sergius. The themes usually pertained to Gospel values, Franciscan life or social justice. These were followed by a period of discussion, after which the dinner guests left. We then proceeded with the weekly community meeting. Here we tried to reach necessary decisions by mutual agreement. The community could be up till the wee hours of the morning trying, after the manner of the Catholic Worker, to reach consensus! Brother Dominic usually sat there looking dead to the world with his head bent over and his shoulders scrunched. However, if you asked him a question about what was going on he could verbalize it: verbatim.

One day a month we had a planned getaway, out of the city and usually to Cedar Lake, Indiana. There was a monastery, a quiet atmosphere, a lake to walk around and a place for Dominic to scrounge for mushrooms. We spent nearly the entire day in silence. Most of us needed the time desperately for the sake of sanity and rejuvenation before returning to the city streets.

There in the jungle of the city we all experienced some horrific moments, like when we saw a nineteen-year-old girl sprawled on the pavement, dead from a drug overdose, or when we threw our arms around Martha, a Puerto Rican mom, who lost the last of her five sons in a gang war. Once we gave hospitality to a youth who, in a suicide attempt jumped in front of the El-train. He had a metal plate inserted the length and width of his forehead. Al lived to recuperate with us and then go on to live a happy, productive married life.

The serious incidents were sometimes juxtaposed with comical ones. There was the day I was trailing far behind Kris who was going up the steps to the El-train only to see her left leg bouncing down the steps toward me and the other commuters. In her haste that morning she failed to strap it on tightly and the cup wasn't a good fit anyway. To many a town bound passenger a leg rolling in their direction was an awesome sight. I caught Kris' limb and hauled it up to the platform. There we sat half laughing, and crying as we strapped her lower leg in place. Another time, Fr. Blase, who also was a mechanic for our two decrepit vehicles, was "on" as community cook for the evening. He came down to our apartment carrying a large serving bowl of orange liquid. Kris, who loved orange jell-O, met him at the door and promptly thrust her finger in the bowl for a taste. Wrong move: What a grimace and a shout followed! Blasé calmly and nonchalantly said: "Transmission fluid."

Two years went by before we realized to what extent the poor were leaving and moving farther north of downtown. A gentrification process was taking place, in which the rich were buying up the properties, pushing out the struggling people and then refurbishing the solid-walled structures to rent them out for big bucks. It was time for us to go too, for we had come to share the fate of the poor.

After long and serious searching we located a place at 903 W. Gordon Terrace where there were a large contingent of Hispanics and Blacks around us and in our building. Life resumed as usual but the atmosphere in the community over the next two years seemed to gradually change. Goals for some of us shifted to further learning and storing up money for higher education; others still wanted the hands on work with the poor. Relationships became divisive and exclusive, making the tension in the house palpable. Added to this, there was marked increase of the noise level from the boom boxes outside, screaming from a half-way shelter for the mentally ill across the street and séances transpiring in an upstairs apartment above the shelter.

All this led me and many of the others to believe that the Spirit was calling us elsewhere. As the tension increased, I realized my need for space, silence and solitude to make an enlightened discernment regarding my next move. A door opened in Arizona. The Carmelites at Nada, who had hermitages in the desert, were willing to let me come and stay in one of them for a month without pay if I would agree to help out part time in cleaning the other guests' hermitages. Soon the Greyhound bus had another passenger; one bound for Sedona.

At Nada half of the days were spent working. The rest of the time was for silence and prayer. The long, warm, starlit nights, the wide open desert space, the stillness and the manual labor — this was a rhythm I loved and thirsted for in my life. But, I was not a Carmelite. I was a Franciscan. Both are Catholic, Christian, Religious Orders seeking to live the Spirit of the Holy Gospel of Christ, but the spirituality, thrust, and way of approaching God is very different. To me the Franciscan way embodies a joyful, outgoing trust in the Creator and a delight in the joys of that creation. Francis seemed to call everything "brother or sister." There is a backward and forward movement from mundane messy earthiness to the transcendent and sublime, finding the footprints of the God-man in it all. Carmelite spirituality seems more distant, less hands on, more taken up with the otherness and hidden aspects of the Godhead.

It was time to make a change and I cried to God: "Lord where? How?"

It was revealed. A friend of a friend was a hermit sister in West Virginia. (A hermit is a person who lives alone for the purpose of being totally devoted to a life of prayer, penance and intercessor for the needs of the world and all his or her brothers and sisters in it). Her name was Sister Joan Sutherland. I knew the terrain of the state as I had been through it as a child on trips to my grandparents, who lived in Coral Gables, Florida. West Virginia had plenty of hills which I hoped would provide a natural solitude, one without the walls of monastic enclosure. In fact, it was closer to St. Francis' way of living: his friars lived in huts in the woods and went out to work. In West Virginia, plenty of poor folks lived close to the earth and worked it. Many of them had a bare minimum of this world's goods but they loved the land and all of creation. I said to myself: "I could live there and have quiet and much time for contemplative prayer. As a nurse I could help care for the folks in their homes. I cannot be sure others will come to share the life with me but, that, I will have to leave up to God."

A letter went out to Sister Joan.

Others were consulted too because this was such a leap. I asked Bishop Hodges, the Ordinary of West Virginia, if he was open to my coming and he referred me back to Sr. Joan requesting that I visit her. I wrote to Father Angelus, the priest my private vows were under and

Fr. encouraged me to: "Give it a go," as did my spiritual director in Chicago. Arky too was a confidant. Arky was an endearing name for one of the Pulaski Franciscan priests who's actual name was Father Arcadius Smolinski. All of us in the Gospel Family revered Arky as a living saint. He had become an itinerant beggar in Europe in the seventies, after the example of St. Francis. Before going there he had tested his vocation in the flop houses of Chicago. One evening while he visited at Gordon Terrace I summoned up the courage to talk to him. I said: "Arky, I am thinking of going to West Virginia as a beggar at first, living alone in the woods and working out part-time among the poor. I long so much for silence, a life of prayer and poverty, and some nursing in the homes of the people. Do you think I am nuts for wanting this?" His piercing eyes bored straight into me as he said forcefully, yet serenely: "Do it! Do it before you are too afraid."

Bishop Hodges had written and said: "Come."

I took off in a little stick shift Chevy and headed for the hills before the voices in my head clamored too loudly that I was out of my mind.

CHAPTER 5

Take Me Home Country Roads

"Praised be to you my Lord for Mother Earth..." St. Francis' Canticle of the Sun

That early October morning in 1976, as I drove away from the "windy city" a few cars were on the ribbon of highway that Fr. Sergius used to dub; the "Damn Ryan." That is what he called Chicago's Dan Ryan Expressway where he could be hung up in traffic for hours. Gentle rain glided over the windshield and tears rolled down my face.

Alone now, I had left behind many very close friends and was heading for a place, I knew not where, in the mountain wilderness of West Virginia. I turned the button of the ole' Chevy radio hoping for some mental diversion. Out over the waves rang the song: "Take Me Home Country Roads." This was immediately followed by another entitled: "You are on the Right Track." Smiling, I mused: How is that for confirmation of a path I felt interiorly compelled to follow?! The track my life had taken so far had been circuitous. It had led in and out of two established religious communities and into urban centers among the disadvantaged. Now, somewhere in my gut was this consuming desire to live simply in solitude and close to nature. Coupled with that was an intense yearning to be alone with the Alone and yet not very far from the country folks whose homes dotted the hollers and hillsides of Appalachia.

Happily enough, the $600 Chevy Vega hummed along the highway. My first long excursion of driving a 'stick' wasn't so bad as long as the map called for roads along interstates of Indiana and Ohio, but as the Appalachian mountain range appeared so too did the challenges. This city gal had to learn fast how to put on the emergency brake, push in the clutch, step gently on the gas, easily release the clutch and ascend in jolts on a nearly vertical plane. Do a few of those maneuvers and the technique can be mastered.

Jesus and Francis had instructed their followers to travel lightly. There was an advantage to not having a car heavily weighted down. The less stuff, the less gas needed - and in fact, all I had was little over a hundred dollars for a room somewhere, a small bag with clothes and a few dishes. Another thing I possessed was an appointment in Wheeling, WV with the Catholic bishop. Bishop Joseph Hodges wanted me to explain to him how I was planning to live the life I envisioned, in his diocese. We had corresponded a few times and he had an idea of what I proposed to do but there was one thing that really troubled me and that was: How do I tell him that I may need to be a beggar at first?

On a clear, crisp, early October morning I located the city of Wheeling on the map and set out to find his office. Figuring that it was probably close to the diocesan cathedral, which was most likely the biggest church in the city, I started looking for steeples and found the right one. The chancery which enclosed the bishop's office was across the street. Treading gingerly up the steps I entered and found the bishop's secretary who ushered me in to his presence.

My knees were shaking and my heart skipped a couple of beats as I surveyed the scene: a huge semi-circular desk towered in papers and behind it sat a figure dressed black with a Roman collar and an Episcopal ring dominating his right hand. He was partially bald and a little rotund. I saw seriousness in his eyes, however, that was complimented by a gentle, welcoming demeanor. I began to relax a bit when he said: "Oh, I'll have to call in the Vicar for Religious." He entered; a rather portly monsignor wearing clerical garb, looking somber, sedate, and rather expressionless as he sat down beside me.

Inside my head I prayed: "Oh God, how am I ever going to get this all out? How do I say I'll be a beggar at first? They will think I am crazy!" Yet this is precisely what I felt the Spirit was calling me to do; to experience once more in our day what it feels like to depend entirely on the providence of God as Jesus and St. Francis had taught.

Bishop Hodges questioned me: "How do you propose to live your life here in this diocese?"

"Nervous and haltingly I began: "I want to live simply and frugally in a place close to the earth and surrounded by the mountains, spending about half a week in silence and stillness and half a week out working among the folks. I envision taking care of the sick in their homes or in whatever work I would find." (Then I knew it was necessary to be completely open and tell about the begging and so I managed to spurt out). "Begging will be necessary at first."

There was a silence, a silence that seemed like eternity.

It was probably more like thirty seconds. Then the bishop said; "Monsignor, what do you think?" More silence…The monsignor slowly put his head down, not uttering a word. With my whole fate wavering in the balance, I waited.

Finally, the bishop spoke saying; "Who am I to stop the Spirit of the Lord? Go ahead."

My heart leapt with joy, for this was the confirmation I needed! God was going to provide as He does for the birds of the air and the lilies of the field. I knelt to receive the bishop's blessing and left his office with a light step and a joyful song in my heart. He had no specific place to send me to so I was free to explore any part, of what the popular singer, John Denver, had dubbed the "almost heaven" state.

That night I received hospitality from Rose Ann. She was a woman who had been an extern (one who is not cloistered but lives just outside the enclosure,) who went on errands, for the Carmelite sisters that had recently lived in Wheeling. She was still staying in the outer quarters of the abandoned monastery and she had plenty of space to share. Later that evening, I was taken on a tour of the inside quarters, so stark and now very desolate. All the little cubicles of the former sisters, the dark narrow hallways, the choir, the refectory, and the community room (that I imagined had once enveloped joyous faces and happy songs), were deserted. Such an aura of sadness came over me there. Having once been a novice in a cloistered community - anticipation was now mounting. Soon my new cloister would be a natural one in the stillness of the mountains, beneath the sun, moon and the stars. The next morning after thanking Rose Ann for her gracious gift of hospitality, the Chevy and I headed south.

Places like Wheeling, WV are not "really" West Virginia in the minds of many people. It is more like a suburb of Pittsburgh: much too much city and with little resemblance to where the majority of the people live, in the hills, hollows and little towns.

Steering the Vega southeast toward Sutton and Gassaway, I came to a halt at Webster Springs where the mountains were so high and the scarce flat land so sequestered by them, I felt cuddled in the warm womb of the earth. That was until I met the pastor of the area. Winding around the little town, I came upon the local Catholic Church and asked to see him. He surely was not only a pastor but a plumber, carpenter, electrician, virtually a jack of all trades. I am sure he helped very many people in the area with his skills. Even as I talked with him he was busy fixing something. Surmising that he would soon be out the door and on the way to another job if I did not lay out my "mission statement" quickly, I speeded up the presentation. When I finished, he said: "You are a nurse and you should be working seventy hours a week. The need is so great."

It did not take much insight to see that he was in no way interested in having someone around who was seeking a life of contemplative prayer and solitude. Nor was I about to locate in a parish where the pastor was not in sympathy with my deepest aspirations. So the Chevy and I did an about face and headed up toward Calhoun County.

Shortly after my arrival there I met some religious sisters who were engaged in social work. One of them was named Sister Marian. After hearing my story she said to me: "Why don't you go over to Roane County and talk to the pastor there? He is Father Dave Glockner, a Glenmary Home Missionary Priest."

Fr. Dave did receive me and he listened kindly and intently to my story. Though he seemed a little hesitant, he mentioned a lady in town, Jean Hershberger, who had a room to rent if I would not mind starting out in a town setting. I acquiesced. He offered to introduce me to her and on his word Jean was gracious enough to let me stay in her little room on the second floor of her house. I gave her the remaining hundred dollars as rent for the ensuing month. Early the next morning and after Mass each day I went out to explore the area, and knock on doors when I was in need of food.

St. Francis had instructed his followers to have recourse to the "table of the Lord" when they found no work. They were to ask for alms for the love of God. There was a scene at the time of Francis, on an occasion where he was very ill. Some knights came to fetch him and on the way back they ran out of food so they went to local houses and offered to buy some. They came back with nothing. Francis sent them out again to the same houses and told them to ask for alms for the love of God and they received and abundance! Francis was trying to get them to trust in the loving providence of God rather than their own "flies," which is the term the saint used for money.

This was a hard act to follow! I had to pray very hard and summon up gobs of courage every time I approached a house. Sometimes I even wished no one was home so I would not be embarrassed.

When the folks saw a rather young woman at the door at the door in a little brown dress and cord around her waist they do not feel intimidated or fearful, just quizzical. After the initial embarrassment I had an opportunity to explain where I came from and what I hoped to do.

The people were so wonderful! They shared their foods; homemade pies, cornbread, dried beans (better known as leather britches,) home canned tomatoes, pickled corn and other delicacies along with their own personal stories and questions. Some folks lived alone and were even anxious to have another person sit down and talk with them. Others wanted to know what I was about and if I planned on staying. It was a good opportunity to do a little evangelization too. Everyone seemed to have heard about the lover of nature and imitator of Christ, St. Francis, but not a one was Catholic.

It all went well until one day, unbeknownst to me, I ended up at a policeman's house and his wife came to the door and shared some food with me while I sat at her table. That night her husband phoned Jean, the lady whose home I was staying in, and said: "If she is living with you why don't you feed her?"

After Mass the next morning Fr. Dave said to me: "Jeanne is there something you would like to talk to me about?" I said:

"No." He replied:

"Well there is something I would like to talk to you about. I got this call last night…" Then he reiterated what my landlady had told him about the policeman's call. Some things had to change. I was not to keep on going around begging in the town. Happily enough Jean knew a lady, a wife of a town lawyer who was looking for a housekeeper and I was hired. That provided money for food. Later I came upon a little old woman who needed some nursing care in her home and that supplied a few more dollars income.

The following November Fr. Dave asked: "Jeanne, are you sure you still want to live alone in a holler?" I replied:

"Oh, yes!" He said:

"I know a fellow who has a house down in Colt Run Holler and he is willing to let someone live in it and care take it for free."

My heart started to skip beats again…intuiting I was coming "home," and indeed I was.

We went out Colt Ridge road to meet with "Archy," aka Bernard Archambeault. The road was one lane and had been paved for about a year. It skirted the top of the mountains with the valleys plummeting far below on either side. From that vantage point one could view vast mountain ranges in the distance. A few modest wooden houses and trailers dotted the scenery on the ridge. Some dwellings were covered with what West Virginians call 'fake brick," which is really glorified tar paper. Smoke from wood stoves swirled out of the chimneys this cool, crisp, day in early November when I was introduced to the Archambeault family; Archy's wife, Fern and their two daughters, Germaine and Sharon. After a cordial introductory conversation I was escorted down the mountainside in back of their place to the valley or holler, known as Colt Run. In early fall the road, all clay, was dry and so down, down we went on a single lane with a precipitous drop off to the right and around a hairpin curve to the left before we took a more gradual descent to the flat land at the bottom. Little did I know that come December this "road" would become impassable even for a Willy's Jeep and in April it would be a mud sucking quagmire after the spring rains. Yes, this is what coming close to Mother Nature meant.

Yet for all the difficulties that "Mother" would ask me to embrace in the coming years, an ineffable peace flooded my spirit that day. As we made the journey down

that woodland path I sensed from somewhere in my deepest self, that after so many years of restless seeking I had
found my niche on this planet. Providence had brought me
"home."

CHAPTER 6

The Cloistered Cabin

"The nurse of full grown souls is solitude." (James R. Lowell)

Sequestered at the bottom of Colt Run Holler, positioned beneath the shadows of soft white pines, there stood an old wooden cabin perched on sand stones. To the right of it was something that looked like the base of an ancient wishing well. To the left, situated precariously on the opposite hillside, was the outhouse. Alongside the cabin about twenty feet away was a creek, known to the local folks as a "crick" and topographically as Colt Run. The quaint structure sported a bay window of sorts. Three panes framed two short needled pines and a holly tree dotted with bright red berries. The view encompassed some rare flat land in the front and in the back of the house. There was no running water. That ancient looking stone circle outside was indeed the well, a dug well- as opposed to what the folks here called a cistern or a drilled well. I could peer way down in it and see the water. A bucket knotted to a rope needed to be plopped down briskly so that it would flop over on its side and become filled. Then a series of strong pulls would draw delicious spring water to the surface. One benefit to this water hauling was that I would not have to worry about frozen pipes during the winter, which was about to bluster its way in.

The path to the outhouse was precarious. Flat stones and small ledges made with a pick axe composed the foot path up the hill to the lop-sided, barn-sided, privy with two holes. I tried to figure out why anyone would build a two holed privy and reasoned that when one side was filled up maybe it could become compost, while the other side was used. Or maybe it was for married couples. It sure was a drafty old place, greatly in need of a door. It helped me to understand why in the old days they used chamber pots at night and perhaps why National Public Radio dubbed their relaxing, restful rhythms as Chamber Music. There is a redeeming factor about outhouses. They have a way of keeping a person in touch with nature; the sounds, sights and smells. All the seasons are appreciated. The path to the outhouse in the spring displays the thousand shades of green bursting forth out of the bleak, somber colored earth. Purple and yellow crocuses poked their heads up and out from under decayed leaves. In summer the breezes vibrated with the music of the cicadas. The fall hosted a swirling mass of magnificent red and gold leaves twirling towards the earth. In winter, nights were often softened by a radiant, starlit sky and moon beams danced on the freshly fallen snow. Without the "comfort station" or the "sheriff's office" as some call it, I would have missed a few of the precious things in life that are free.

Many of the older houses constructed in Appalachia are Jenny Lyn by design, which essentially means they have no insulation. You can sink a nail anywhere without having to worry about it hitting airspace. In my house I had to drill a hole first, into the seasoned oak behind the horse-hair-type wall board and then sink a nail.

There were four rooms in this one story house: a kitchen, living room, two bedrooms and no bath. The floor had a ripple effect and I felt that the post in the center of the house was responsible for keeping the whole structure upright. In the kitchen the sink had a black sewage pipe line straight out to the creek. Next to the sink was an International Harvester refrigerator. I remember thinking, when I first saw it, that the only things International Harvester ever manufactured were tractors. The old contraption lasted for years and years. I almost hoped it would die so I could get something else because the freezer was the size of a shoe box.

Part of the kitchen furniture was an old, pea green colored, wooden table with two chairs. One day I came home from working in town to see a huge black circular ring in the middle of it. There was nothing on that table when I had left in the morning. As I drew closer I gasped. It was a fat, long black snake just sunning itself in my dining area! Once I got over the initial fright and felt grateful that it was not a copperhead I ran for a hoe. In that moment my dad's instructions of many years ago were a godsend. The snake wrapped around the hoe and I speedily got it out the door and far away. Now I knew why folks have cats and dogs and mothballs. Snakes don't like the smell of those balls strewn around the outside of the home and they will shy away – most of the time.

In the living room was a brown, plastic covered couch propped up on old, white enamel range legs and not far from it was a wood stove (what we call a tin Lizzy). Made of tin, it heats up very speedily and burns a hot fire but then just as speedily (like at 2:00 am,) it is cold as the winter air outside. Wood fires were one of the first big challenges to surviving on Colt Run.

Winter would soon be here. It was November and the winds were beginning to howl. The air whistled cold around and under the ill fitting doors and window frames that had shrunken with age. I had to become knowledge-able about kindlin' wood which sets the fire ablaze. Luckily for me Jack brought a huge bundle of it down to the hollow in his "Ford."

I piled the small sticks of wood neatly at a safe distance from tin Lizzy. That November night, which was frigid, I burnt nearly all of it trying to keep the place heated. A few days later Jack was back to see how I was doing and soon he exclaimed: "What happened to all the kindlin'?!"

"Well, I burned it in an effort to stay warm." I said. His eyes lit up in disbelief! He exclaimed:

"That is only to start the fire. You have to put larger logs on top of it and damper it down once they are burning.

The next in-service was on how to regulate the draft and the damper, which was followed by my first lesson in how to use a chain saw to get those larger logs. Jack began the instruction. Rapid fire directions flowed out of his mouth as he bent over and clicked a lever. "Start it like this. Pull the choke out. Turn the power switch up. Depress the gas lever. Yank the rope. Hold the bar and chain away from you." I struggled to follow and remember the sequence as I trailed behind him in his steel toed boots, gray workman's pants, faded plaid jacket, balding head, and buzzing saw, over to a large hardwood tree. Then more directions tumbled out of his mouth. "Notch the tree in the direction it might be leaning and in which you want it to fall. By the way, oak and hickory are the best for a good hot fire. Pine will clog the chimney with sap, especially if it is green. Walnut and maple will not produce much heat. Make sure there is plenty of free space around the bottom of the tree so you can move quickly away if you have to. Spread your feet apart for balance. Do not let the end of the chain bar come in contact with anything as it will buck back. If the chain runs into an old nail, fencing wire, or touches the ground, the cutting teeth will be dulled." The teaching process continued until we had to stop to refuel the saw with the mixed gas and chain bar oil. All of a sudden Jack got very still and pensive. He looked up at the clear blue autumn sky and the tall, soft needled, swaying white pines on the hillside above us and asked in awe: "Can't you hear God whisperin' in them trees?" I nodded:

"Yes," and then went on to think: This fellow, hidden in the hills of West Virginia, is not far from the Creator and closely tuned into the Spirit.

Early on in winter, weary from sawing logs and stacking timber, I went to our little parish church for Mass. The section of the liturgy when we prayed the, "Our Father..." I substituted the words: "wood supply" for "daily bread." After Mass I was dumbfounded when Father Dave called me aside and said: "Jeanne, I got a call from Richard Cronin last night and he told me that he is bringing you a truckload of sawed up wood today."

That type of thing was to happen over and over again these first years in WV. I'd go away to work and there would be a bag of homegrown fruits or veggies on my doorstep when I got home, or I would need something and it would just appear without my having mentioned a word to anyone. Who, given these circumstances, would not be reminded of the words of the Gospel? "So do not worry; do not say, "What are we to eat? What are we to drink? How are we to be clothed? Your heavenly Father knows you need them all. Set your hearts on his kingdom first, and on his righteousness and all these other things will be given you as well. So do not worry about tomorrow; tomorrow will take care of its self."

Winter brought with it a deeper measure of solitude. That is when everything seems to hibernate and holler roads are often non-negotiable. Snuggling by a wood fire with a good book and a cup of coffee, taking long walks in a pristine wilderness of white snow, peering out my cabin window at a full moon on a starlit night and seeing deer trekking through the tree shadowed silhouettes on the mountainside – all this communion with creation enabled a deep peace to infiltrate my soul.

I had been led to a cloister. It was one not provided by convent or monastery walls. There was a "grand silence," as we used to call it in the convent, not circumscribed by bells. There was no one else around my "cell," except the four legged ones of squirrel, possum, raccoon, rabbits and such.

According to ancient practice I prayed the monastic hours, or Office of Morning Prayer and Evensong, and I read the Sacred Scripture, but, all without a definite time-line. If I wanted a few hours to savor a particular passage and rest in it, I could. The monastic life teaches self-discipline, how to live with others and how to structure the days. It provided me the very necessary groundwork for the solitary life. However this life of solitude allowed me to more easily savor the Word and gave me time to just sit with It. The emphasis was on "being," being present to all that just is and not having to "be" anywhere.

For a very long time I could not understand why I did not "fit" in a Franciscan religious institution when I so much wanted to and there was so much agony in leaving them. I discovered that some "soul-scapes" are just not created for them. Some souls are misfits. Some souls need wilderness.

CHAPTER **7**

Life on Colt Run

"Day by day, stone by stone build your secret slowly. Day by day you'll grow too you'll know heaven's glory." (Movie: Brother Sun and Sister Moon.)

Just as things were beginning to fall into place: how to keep the wood fires going with the right kind of timber, what seeds to plant in a garden and when, what soils were alkaline or acidic, what to do with baked clay sod to make it produce – Boom! Comes the revelation that my landlord, Archy, is selling the cabin and property and it will be necessary for me to leave by early spring.

"Jesus!" I cried: "I know we have to be detached from everything, but so soon, and now what?!"

Archy must have felt a little remorse at asking me to leave quickly because a few days later he came to the house and said: "Let's go talk to Gay Vannest. He lives in town with his wife Alice and they own the property next to mine down there on Colt Run. They have not lived on it for ages." So off we went to see the elderly, childless couple. Gay had been a policeman for the town of Spencer many years back and was now retired. He had quite a reputation for honesty. It was said that once when he parked in the city parking lot, the meter ran out and he gave himself a ticket. He also made the rounds of all the businesses in town in the early evening and checked to see that the doors were locked for the night. If they were not, the proprietor would certainly be notified. Gay had a heart for animals, especially the stray dogs. He used to bring the canines home, I was told, and he situated them on the hills around the house. Then he would lug one hundred pound feed bags out over the ridge and down to the holler to nourish them.

His wife Alice, on the other hand, had been used to city life. She was tall, slender, and stylish. Her sharp features, blemish-free skin and gray hair brushed up in a bouffant sweep gave her a queenly air. She hailed from Keyser, WV, closer to Maryland, where she would have seen an influx of city culture. Alice had been a telephone operator before she married Gay.

Living in a holler, alone all day, with the chickens, other fowl, dogs yipping on hills while she tried to clean, cook, and keep a fire going were not her ideas of a happy married life. Gay would return late in the evening and be off again early next morning. Finally having had enough of this, Alice found a job, in the town of Spencer, as a clerk in the Super K Market and one day issued her husband an ultimatum: "I'm going to live in town: Now you can either come and join me or stay where you are."

He came. The little four room house on Colt Run was abandoned that day as well as many of the things in it.

Now, twenty-five years later Archy and I were sitting with them in their tiny apartment in town. Gay said he was willing to let me live in their old house rent free for three years for fixing it up and care-taking it. So the deal was struck and the paper signed. Town folk had assured me that Mr. Vannest was a person to keep his word and he did.

A house in a WV holler doesn't just sit there quietly vacant for a quarter of a century without intrusion: exploration, burglary, vandalism, and dry rot. All crossed the threshold. If it had not been for the tin roof keeping out most of the rain, it would have collapsed. Not a window pane remained. The front door was gone while the back one swung eerily in the wind on a single hinge. A three foot by five foot piece, of horse hair type sheet rock, was gouged out of the wall between two of the rooms.

It was said of St. Francis that he told his friars to build their houses small, and their cells of wood, not stone. He didn't want his brothers living in any elaborate structures.

It seemed to me that the Poverello would have loved this place. So the work to make it a home began. I'd spend the day fixing and repairing here and then traipse over to the other house at night to sleep.

Gay had a habit of collecting newspapers. Stacks of them filled the entire house. They were from various cities in the United States, dating as far back as 1917. Strewn among them were canning jars, and shards of glass bottles from a bygone era. Folks up on the ridge soon got word of the daunting task I had in clearing out and repairing the place and in their goodness and generosity they came down and helped. What a bonfire those papers and debris made!

In the kitchen one could look through the ceiling at the north eastern corner and see the sky. Beneath that stood an old electric range that had caught the snow for twenty-five years. Originally Archy and I tossed it over a nearby hill believing that it could never be functional after all that time, but then again I had no stove. So...later we brought it back into the house, plugged the cord in and it worked; oven and all! Over in the far corner of the kitchen the donated International Harvester Refrigerator stood proudly humming away.

The rats, in years gone by, had a hey-day gnawing circular holes in the living room floor. The kitchen flooring sagged in the center like an old mattress. Consequently, the kitchen table had a decided tilt. The cheapest way to replace the floor was with what was called: "press board," saw dust glued into solid sheets. With help from Jack, Archy and some of the kids up on Colt Ridge, we were able to get the boards into place. That very night rain poured down in torrents right through the holes in the tin roof above and I spent all the nocturnal hours with a mop and a bucket trying to keep the floor from disintegrating into gooey muck. In the wee morning moments I cried to God for help, discouraged and in tears: "Lord where are You?!" It was a piercing petition I would reiterate over and over again. I would pray and strength would come to keep on going. It was a daunting task. Alone, I certainly did not have the interior reserves of resolution and determination or the exterior reserves of strength or capitol.

Jack had an ingenious technique for spotting and patching holes in a tin roof. Again he lent a helping hand. From the inside he had me stick a piece of straw up through any of the holes I noticed then he would go outside and climb up on the roof with a bucket of black tar pitch and a wide paint brush and cover all the holes with straws sticking out of them. He saved the kitchen floor.

A very important step on my agenda was to find the

well. I hunted days for it. Surely, I thought Alice and Gay had to have a source of water besides the creek running along the back yard that was dry as dust through the entire summer. After diligent searching with no results I made a visit to town to ask Alice where the well was. Looking surprised, she said: "It is right out the back door a few feet."

So were the ancient, twisted Concord grape vines, the masses of prickly multi-flora roses and more papers, bottles and debris. One day to my sheer delight I located it. The opening lay under a large flat rock obscured by heaps of refuse. I saw the six-inch circular hole of the cylinder well. Peering down that long tube into the ground there was some shiny liquid I could see many feet below. Now what? Time had come for an in-service on an aluminum bailer. One could be purchased down at McIntosh hardware for nine or ten dollars. The device was cylindrical in shape, about four inches wide and four feet long, with a handle at the top to which a long rope was attached. A trap lever was situated inside at the bottom. A person had to lower the whole mechanism far down into the well. The water in the well would cause the trap lever to rise and the bailer would fill. When it was filled the force of the fluid held the lever down sealing the liquid in. The last step was to pull up on the rope till the bailer was out of the hole, hold it over a bucket, lift up on the trap door and presto, water filled your pail! St. Francis used to describe water as fair, precious and chaste. Truly Brother Francis, truly!

An old root cellar, topped by a smoke house, topped by another holey tin roof sat disintegrating on the other side of the well. It is a style of building common to many old rural homesteads in Appalachia. I smiled as I contemplated the ingenuity and industriousness of the early settlers. Like the family dwelling, the smoke house was also a Jenny Lyn structure, but without any inside paneling. All along the walls on the far side were lined huge spikes which had been hammered into the oak boards. On these spikes they hung the "processed" meats for the homestead. Beef and pork would have been salted and smoked out there. Beneath the flooring of the smoke house was the family's root cellar – dug into the earth, walled with stones, covered with layers of whitewash, (a lime and water preparation) and lined with canning shelves. The flooring was cement with a drain in the center and a red clay pipe under the floor to take any in-seeping water out to the creek. Here in the cellar things like eggs, milk, cheese and the like were kept cool and canned goods would never freeze. In fact to prove the point there were Mason jars on a top ledge filled with canned blackberries from a quarter of a century ago.

Outhouses were strategically placed. I learned that sometime later when trying to establish a hole myself. At certain locations they collect ground water when it rains, or the red clay can be of such density as to absorb absolutely nothing. It is simply dangerous and miserable to evacuate over that. A person could imagine what might happen to the well water if one is stupid enough to place a hole anywhere nearby on level ground or above it. My outhouse, I was informed, was a Teddy Roosevelt structure. During the Great Depression work parties were initiated by the government to stimulate the economy. In this one holed shanty the back rest was shaped in the form of a T for Teddy. Later, when I did do some home health nursing in certain rural parts of the county, I found the same T's all over the place.

Some types of manure seem next to miraculous. About

fifty feet away from the privy, up on a level stretch, Gay and Alice had a chicken coup which was in a state of total collapse. Those ancient old oak boards, I reflected, would make terrific kindlin' wood, so with the chain saw and axe I stashed a fine pile of starter wood for the next winter. The soil under that old fowl house was a black, rich, loam. Mostly, for the fun of it, I took a sampling down to the county extension office and the results came back: "highest in every nutrient." I had just located the first garden spot. The spinach and lettuce leaves were a foot high that year. Asparagus was a challenge; I had the locals laughing at me when they learned it was planted upside down. I was not the only greenhorn in the community: One of the surgeons asked a patient of his why he only got one cabbage off a cabbage plant; a teaching moment. Another time all the tomato plants just drooped over and died on July 4. Highly dismayed I trotted into the county extension office once more, this time with a straggly stalk of tomato plant and asked: "What happened?" The agent looked at me sheepishly and said:

"Did you plant your tomato plants anywhere near black walnut trees?"

"Yes." I told him: "There are two of those huge trees bordering the garden." He replied:

"There's your problem. The tannic acid in the soil from those trees kills the tomato plants."

Being so upset about the ruined garden, I chain sawed down the walnut trees. My woes were not over. One falling tree took down the electric line. The stack of walnut firewood brought comments like: "You are using good black walnut for firewood: How could you?!"

Stacking winter wood inside an old shed attached to the

back of the house was another blunder. The room adjacent to the shed, on the inside of the house was a tiny eight foot by ten foot room. I used it as a prayer and meditation space where it was easy to be quietly alone and tranquil in the presence of the Lord. One day, behind me, just on the other side of the wall, I heard a horrible loud clatter and commotion in the wood shed. Shuddering, I gingerly got up, tiptoed out the back door and peeked inside the shed. Two long, fat, black snakes were wound round each other, copulating. Up, down and over the stacks of wood they gyrated. Feeling like a murderer I put an end to their reverie – with a hoe. Blood was everywhere.

When some days later I told Jack about it, he commented, with a look of astonishment written all over his face as he asked: "Why did you kill the black snakes? They eat the copperheads." Just what a person needed to hear.

Termites and cockroaches love wood piles too. I had noticed the termites and thought just for the heck of it I would call an exterminator and get an estimate of how much it would cost to "get shed" of the termites. Down to the holler he came with his truck and gear. He spent twenty minutes walking around the house figuring and speculating. At long last he came up with an estimate of $600. I told him: "Why, Sir the house isn't worth that much!" He understood and left quietly.

A lesson was learned that day. Termites have to have contact with wood or earth. If there is one place where the frame house is in contact with the ground that site is a termite's port of entry. That is why early settlers strategically placed huge old sandstones to support the house up off the ground.

Just after stacking all that firewood it needed re-stacking somewhere else away from the living space. St. Francis taught his brothers in one of his admonitions: You can never tell how patient or humble a person is when all is going well with them. It seems that the big challenges in life don't call for as much heroism as those Murphy's Law days, the ones no one notices, the daily grind with the million and one things that can go wrong and get under our skin. They seem to push by inches to a precipice where we can either choose to fall off or fly.

A couple of months passed before the dilapidated dwelling had scrubbed walls with fresh bright paint. The window spaces sported newly caulked frames and shiny glass panes. The patched roof ceased leaking and the kitchen floor was covered with a piece of new, speckled linoleum which the locals call a "rug." A tiny barrel drum stove kept the room delightfully warm. The meditation space was my joy. It had a small altar situated beneath a suspended San Damiano Crucifix, (a replica of the cross,) under which St. Francis heard the commission of Christ: "Go rebuild my church." As twilight descended, the altar candle lights sent soft shadows dancing on the walls. The spiraling, sandalwood incense wafted its fragrance up toward the crucifix and then back toward a small earthling sitting on a prayer bench, ever so grateful and happy to be exactly where she was.

.

CHAPTER **8**

Alone with the Alone

"Be still and know that I am God." (Ps. 46:10)

Christianity has a place for misfits; and some go way back in time to 300-400AD, the age of the desert Fathers and Mothers; for example, Abbas and Ammas fled a very materialistic, consumer driven society to live in the desert in an attempt to commune more easily with God and to intercede for their fellow men and women. They went to pray and…do battle. Laura Swan speaks of these Ammas in her book, The Forgotten Desert Mothers. The women knew they were doing battle in the wilderness. It was a place of death – the place to die to the false self and false supports, to bury old ways and attitudes. It was the realm of the spiritual and demonic.

The Ammas went to places such as the deserts of Egypt, Syria, Persia and present-day Turkey. They were found all around the Mediterranean world, northward into Gaul (France), and later into Ireland and Britain. Favored sites were often within a day's walk of a small village in order to maintain some contact outside the community.

Desert ascetics believed that the greatest enemies of the inner journey were hurry, crowds and noise. The desert was a place for silencing the inner racket that kept them from hearing the whispers of God. They chose to dwell alone in the quietude with freedom to be totally open to the Source of all life.

The Abbas and Ammas discovered it was very hard for the human spirit to penetrate to the Truth when life is loaded down with cares, possessions, and numerous activities. Status symbols meant nothing; for whom was there to feel important in front of? What good was wealth? There was nothing to buy. As for control, who was there to control? What needed control or restraints were the passions within one's own heart as they came face to face with the evil and demonic forces that assailed them. The solitaries came to realize their total dependence on the Creator and to learn of that Creator's individual love for them in a way that was profoundly experiential.

As much as I wanted to learn about the Appalachian folks and their rural culture, my deepest desire was to find the Face and embrace of God in the wilderness cloister of the mountains. Folks did ask: "Don't you get awfully lonely living down there by yourself?" Basically my answer was:

"No." There were times I was eager for some human companionship, but on the whole it needs to be pointed out that there is a great difference between living a lonely life and a solitary life. The lonely person is essentially a sad person and an unfulfilled person. One following a true call to solitude finds in it their deepest joy. There are down days, but taken as a whole I found the life of the solitude to be one of deep contentment, vibrant with life and a sense of purpose. For the person called to this vocation knows that he or she is certainly not in it for themselves. They know intuitively that the closer they draw to the Source, the closer they are to their brothers and sisters in this world. They are day and night before that God in the prayer of simple presence, adoration and petition for the needs of all humankind. This, combined with a life of simple manual labor, spiritual reading, lectio (prayerful pondering of Scripture), and a frugal lifestyle helped them to enter into the silence where they could be attuned to the answers of the All Holy One. That is why so many solitaries in the past had people coming to the far-away places seeking them out for the wisdom they could share and the guidance they could give so well. This is not easily understood, especially in a culture that is so fast-paced and goal oriented as ours.

A moment of insight came one day as I let a bucket flop down into the well outside the house. What if the well went dry and there was no water to be had? How utterly essential to my existence here in the hollow was that underground spring?! Following upon that was the thought: What happens when the inner well runs dry? How does the life flow get back in? That is what the life in solitude is about: tapping the Source and sharing it with others. The difficulty comes when the Source decides it is time to play hide and seek in order to be more deeply found. Then a solitary is up against the desert dryness, called "acedia." Only persistent prayer and a good spiritual director can help with the aridity and temptations that inevitably arise.

In communion with God and seeking the advice of a spiritual mentor (for me it was Father Angelus), who knew the whole spiritual labyrinth of my vocation, I found the way to go on in joy. The strength was given to put one foot in front of the other, to keep on keeping on when oc-currences in my spirit or the world around me screamed: "Defeated!"

When one is alone, without much outer distracting stimulation, the shadow sides of the personality can and often do rear up to stare us in the face. There is no easy escape unless we become very busy and ignore the call to quiet contemplation and immersion in the Word. We often use masks (or Personas), to evade what we are really and thus impede the healing process that has to go on. There is a diamond in each of us but it gets awfully obscured with crud over the years and it is painful to have that crud scrubbed off by inner work.

Sometimes I felt drawn to just sit very still and let the Spirit wash over me like a tidal wave. Other days I felt a sense of buoyancy lifting my soul up and over the rough waters below. In the spring there was the experience of "going with the flow," like the gurgling stream outside the kitchen window that cradled a leaf and carried it along. Occasionally, I seemed to be on the bottom of a dry well and stuck in the mud with walls all around and no one to help. The only chance I had was to cry out and wait for the rescue, and in the stillness the rescue came.

One frigidly cold, winter day, feeling lonely, I tried to keep warm on the old brown plastic couch. All of a sudden a warm presence overshadowed me and before my mind's eye floated the scene of a very small child, who was alive and well, yet wrapped in a mummy dressing from head to toe. I was that small child and I could not see or move and yet I was convinced beyond all doubt that I was being loved, rocked and held in the arms of God.

In an exasperating moment I headed for a far lonely

meadow and shouted at the top of my lungs: "Where are you God!?" It was one of those days when nothing was making too much sense and Murphy's Law seemed to have kicked into full gear. I felt I could understand neither the why or wherefore of events as they were unfolding. The solitude had yet to teach me experientially that as long as we think we can do or "fix" anything about ourselves, by ourselves, we go back to the first rung of the spiritual ladder.

Bishop Hodges had given me permission to have the Blessed Sacrament at the cabin in a special room. One day I interiorly intuited a sense of battle. While in prayer before the Lord I seemed to have a very strong sense of His Presence and the words that came to me were: "I want you very much." Then it was as if some very dark, cold, unseen, force, entered the room and spoke very emphatically:

"And so do I!" It left me with a chill and prickly flesh.

Not that it would ever be possible to prove to anyone that experience, but to this day the effect of that encounter lingers and convinces me that those who live in prayerful solitude do battle not only with inner forces.

Our bishop had been glad that I was simply garbed in a little brown dress with a cord around my waist and a thin silver band on my ring finger signifying my promise of celibacy. He told me to use the title: "Sister" even though I was not a member of an official religious community, but only under private vows. He explained: "Folks are not going to understand why you are living alone in a hollow."

For the most part he was right. There was at least one exception. Mr. Orville Barker, an older gentleman who lived up on the Ridge said to me one day: "Jeanne many folks around here do not know why you are living all alone down there on Colt Run, but I do." Then, I said with bated breath:

"Why am I living down there Mr. Barker?" His reply brought tears to my eyes and goose bumps to my flesh. Orville, who had no background knowledge of the solitary vocation, profoundly intuited the concept when he replied:

"You are down there for us."

CHAPTER 9

Greening

"If you keep a green bough in your heart, a singing bird will come."
(Ancient Chinese proverb).

Shortly after his conversion, St. Francis spent several years living as a hermit, and although he and his friars chose the mixed life of prayer and apostolic activity he often went to hidden places to pray. Francis wanted to have within his order places that the friars could go to from time to time to live in a solitary way. Within the enclosure of the little group, of no more than four, each one was to have a place for himself so he would not be forced to live or sleep with the others.

One such "loci" or place is still well known today, and that is the Carceri, which is located high on Mount Subasio above the town of Assisi. The sounds of the city cannot be heard there. Huge boulder rocks bolster the steep formidable landscape with its alternating moods. At times gentle breezes waft their way through the undulating arms of verdant branches and the heavens are a dome of a clear and azure blue. Then, at any given moment the winds can take up howling as the trees respond in frenzied swirls. The deep gray sky is split with lightning bolts and mother earth trembles beneath the assault of thunder gone wild. The elements seem to roar with a ferocious might or express the tender caress of enfolding arms. Francis had a small cave here.

Colt Run Holler, though not a high mountain fastness, shares the wild and wonderfulness of a Mount Subasio with its boulder rocks, jagged outcroppings, and its mini waterfalls in spring. Lightning dances off of tin roofs. Thunder clapping rattles shed doors and white pines sway gracefully through it all.

Francis' idea of the hermetical life and his consequent, "Rule for Hermitages," resonated so deeply in me because it allowed for protracted periods of silence, prayer and simple manual labor with no bells or telephones. My hope was to have something like that one day. Of course no man-made enclosures of hedges would be needed where I was. Here, were enough hills and a multiplicity of multiflora rosebushes to ensure any person's private space.

As I envisioned it, the place would include the main house with a chapel, a communal laundry, phone, gathering space, a community garden and then several cabins in the surrounding hills; places for solitary living in prayer, simplicity, silence and doing the labor of crafts…There would be a common fund and as many as two or three days a week could be spent out and around the county in a working ministry to help others and to provide for our material needs. Always, however, the emphasis of our life would be on solitude and seeking the Face of God.

Before long I was introduced to two individuals; Tricia Russell and Tom Gagnon, who were actively and seriously seeking a more intense following of the Gospel life. Tricia lived with her husband, Tony about twenty-five miles away in Tanner, WV. Their rustic, weathered wood home graced an almost inaccessible hilltop deep in the woods. One day I went to the Russell's house for a visit. The family truck rocked over the boulders and lunged forward in spurts as I sat half paralyzed in the front seat, while Tony negotiated the poorest excuse of a road I had ever seen. Tricia and I became close friends and periodically she would come over to Colt Run for discussions on the spiritual life.

Tom Gagnon had been a lay volunteer with a home missionary society and had heard about the life I was leading in the holler. He stopped by one day for a visit and before I knew it he made a decision to leave his home in Fort Pierce, FL and to take up residence in Roane County. Tom, being an excellent carpenter, decided he too wanted to live simply in the spirit of the Gospel and of St. Francis. Before long he got permission from some of the folks to build a little wooden hut among the trees above the town of Spencer.

One day Tom, with his muscular physique, tanned skin and auburn Afro-frizzed curly locks took the "mandatum" or mandate of Christ to the young man in the Gospel very seriously and went to sell all his possessions. Then he took the money in one hundred dollar bills and proceeded to go door to door passing them out to the poor up on the hill where he was living. The stunned folks just did not know what to think of it and they called the police on him suspecting they might have a lunatic in their midst. The perplexed officers were in a quandary. They were unable to prove it wasn't his own money he was distributing. No charges stuck and the folks on the mountain soon came to know Tom as "brother." They took him into their hearts and homes. He helped them with odd jobs, especially those projects needing carpentry skills and he also came down to the holler on Colt Run to exercise his building expertise, which was accepted with deep gratitude.

At the beginning of my fourth year in Colt Run Holler I began to earnestly ask the Lord: "Please send a sister companion to share this type of Franciscan life with me." One day, in the dead of winter, shortly after this request had been made a singing bird, a bright red cardinal, would alight and perch on the ancient Rose of Sharon bush outside the kitchen window. He kept chirping and crashing himself against the pane. Every day this would happen. I couldn't help thinking about the Chinese proverb and asking: "Could this be a harbinger of something exciting about to occur?" I knew birds do crash into windows when they see their reflection in them but this bird never stopped. The gaily feathered creature stirred something in my depths and tapped an inner well where words could not express the intimation and anticipation that bubbled up inside.

Then one evening after this determined avian persistence had gone on for quite some time a phone call came. "Is this Jeanne?"

"Yes:" I responded. The caller identified herself as Sister Jane from Ohio. We had never met, but she explained that we had a mutual friend, a Sister Miriam Friday from Chicago. Miriam and I had worked together in the inner city in the 1970's and Jane had visited her there quite recently. Jane, in her mid-thirties, was hoping to locate to Appalachia. Until then she had spent much of her life as a Franciscan Sister as a high school teacher in Ohio. She had headed up an alternative school for problem kids, which led her into a temporary case of blues and burnout when it was decided the school had to close. She had taken some time out, delved into pottery and gone to a house of prayer for a year. Now she felt she was being led to live simply, poorly and prayerfully in a rural area. Jane said to me: "Miriam told me about you and your situation there. Do you think I could come for a visit?"

My heart skipped a beat and then I said: "Sure." A short while later we spent some hours sharing as the evening candle and its light waned to a stub. Jane was very much attracted to this setting and lifestyle. We had much in common; a Franciscan background, a love for the poor and the desire to embrace a very simple lifestyle. We wanted to live quietly and prayerfully, close to the earth, raising a garden, doing some part-time ministry. Miriam even entertained the thought of coming to dwell in the holler and did visit but, then finally decided that she was meant to live in Chicago in transient hotels with the homeless.

Jane talked to her community in Ohio and began a discernment process with the sisters of her community. It was determined that yes, Jane would come to WV. So one blustery March day as the wind whipped over Colt Ridge, Jane arrived, escorted by Sisters Gemma and Tanya. They walked down into Colt Run Holler because that is how Jane first wanted to experience her new home. The road was red clay mud, and rutted. The last day of winter was chilly, clear and crisp. As the trio arrived I threw the front door open; my heart full of expectancy and joy. Later we ascended to the ridge to get Jane's belongings. My heart sank as I saw all the stuff she brought with her. There were teaching and artist supplies and some memorabilia from her motherhouse. To her I guess it was not much. I had asked her to come poor and she really thought she did. However, there was more in that car than I had when coming to WV with not even a place to lay my head and I reacted and overreacted, I guess. St. Francis had insisted that his first brothers leave all behind when they came to the Order and I was hoping for the same kind of trust. Jane was very hurt when I said a lot of things weren't necessary and needed to go back to Ohio. It did not make for a smooth beginning and it all was, in fact, a glimmer of the intense struggles we would face for many years down the road from that March day in 1980.

Tom had quickly constructed a dividing wall in the one and only small bedroom in the house using two-by-fours covered on either side by paneling. So in each space there was scarcely room enough for a single bed, chair and night stand. We managed as best we could and that wasn't always very well. One day I remember mixing some old yogurt and Ranch salad dressing together and I topped our green salad for supper with it. That was a recipe for disaster. We both got purged. Each of us had a five gallon plastic bucket in our tight quarters for the diarrhea and vomiting that ensued all night long and through the next day. Oh, the smell! Then someone tipped off our rather fastidious, but loving and generous pastor, Father Rollie, that we were sick and he came, as a true Glenmarian (Glenmarians are home missionary priests and brothers serving in rural America), hoofing it down the slick, icy mountain path toting a backpack with gifts for us: toilet paper and ginger ale. He entered the house but was leery of looking at two "nuns" in bed so he averted his eyes while talking to us. He left in a few moments, after giving us a blessing and expressing his wishes for our renewed health. How we laughed!

Our life together at the beginning had a simple rhythm. We would each rise early to spend time in quiet meditation. That would be followed by the Office, which is the liturgical prayer of the whole church, composed mainly of psalms from the bible and canticles and short readings from the Sacred Scriptures. We would go to early Mass at our parish church; Holy Redeemer, and then come home for breakfast and the beginning of the day's work. In the evenings we would again pray the Office of the day and have supper together. A lot of our work was done alone then except for the two or three days a week out in the town.

The old shed in back of the house that had served as a smoke house was transformed into a pottery where

Jane would spend hours wedging the clay and spinning the potter's wheel to form beautifully crafted wares. She also started a pre-school named the Pumpkin Patch which met in the basement of the rectory at the church two or three days a week. Though it brought in very little income, her teaching met with great success.

Both of us worked the land, although it took Jane awhile to get into the gardening and canning. We both cut and hauled in the winter wood supply. One day a week we went over to the Spencer State Hospital for the mentally ill and volunteered our time in visiting and feeding the residents.

Tom would come and work on the building projects: a barn to store the wood, a rustic chapel for communal prayer and the beginning of a couple of small hermitages. Almost all our boards were rough cut lumber donated from Tom McLaughlin's saw mill or second time around materials from wherever we could scrounge them. Tom was a genius at putting it all together. I tried nursing in the homes, free-lancing it, but that endeavor met with meager success as the folks were needy but unable to pay for services or supplies. Some money was necessary for our self support so I did housekeeping jobs trying to steer away from professionalism. In the end, however, I missed nursing the sick and applied for two or three days a week job at our little local hospital. They hired me. At Roane General there was no such thing as specialty nursing. All the nurses worked all the departments: OB, Peds, Med-Surge, ICU, and ER. Here is where I learned so much more about the people and the county and its doctors.

One winter around Christmas a rough looking, paint peeling, brown van pulled up in front of our house and out climbed a motley crew. They introduced themselves as: Indian Bob, Bear, Dakota, Arizona, and, I believe her name was Grace. They told us they were from Arizona and intended to take up homesteading in the house up our holler which had been vacant for some months. They intended to grow blue corn for a livelihood. The group had hardly anything in the way of supplies. Indian Bob was the father, a Black Foot Native American raised in a Catholic nun's orphanage as a child. He said: "This place really impresses me. Never seen no nuns living like this before." Bear was his wife and she was from an Apache reservation in the southwest. Dakota was their six-month old infant with round face and straight jet black, shiny hair, parted down the middle. Arizona and Grace, I believe, had some type of relationship but, were not married. On Christmas Day we offered to fix supper for them. Indian Bob even came over and helped with the preparation and mashed the potatoes. Everyone seemed grateful to have had a good meal with all the trimmings and a warm house to relax in. Jane and I felt we had our own Appalachian version of the Nativity scenario. Then the inevitable happened.

One night the baby caught a fever. He was miserable and his nose was filled with mucus. His black hair kept falling over his eyes and into the nasal discharge. Jane decided to cut a lock of the hair to get it out of the way and this caused a tirade with the father. He screamed: "You NEVER cut an Indian's hair!" Jane apologized. She really didn't realize it was taboo. We surmised this action touched a raw nerve from the days when Indian Bob was in the orphanage and tribal customs meant little to the nuns who cared for him.

Grace was awfully congested too, and the stethoscope told my ears that both of them were really sick. Of course none of them had any health insurance. The next morning I had to work a shift at the hospital so I had them sign in at Doctor Pedro Ambrosio's office. Pedro was one of our doctors who rarely ever refused anybody care, so, I hedged it was a safe bet to send them there. It wasn't long after this decision that I heard my name paged over the hospital system. "Sister Jeanne 202! Sister Jeanne 202!" Rapidly, I dialed the number knowing full well it was Doctor Ambrosio's extension. I heard his voice come bellowing through the phone: "Seeeeester! Who are these people you sent to my office?! They will not even give me their last names. So, how can I treat them? They have pneumonia but it is illegal to prescribe for someone without proper identification."

I will never know what he did, but at any rate, they got the care they needed and were cured. It was not long after that episode they decided; maybe trying to locate a place in Appalachia, in the dead of winter, with an infant and without supplies was unwise. One February day they took off in the old brown van. It clamored out of the holler wrenching and sputtering. The exhaust pipe was belching smoke and a few flames. We never heard from them again.

One spring afternoon Jane and I returned from being out in the town to find that someone had tampered with the Blessed Sacrament in our chapel. The Sacred Species was locked into a little brown rectangular box that we call a tabernacle. It had a sunburst clay inset on the front panel, and sat on the altar. The lock piece was bent and on seeing it I became nervous and upset. Also, there was some food missing from the kitchen. Both Jane and I had a very good idea who did it. We had befriended a family up on Colt Ridge which was very poor. Their house was in shambles. The boys were abused by an alcoholic father. Often they were in trouble with the law. When two of them were confronted by us, they did not deny they did it. The kids thought since there was this special box with a perpetual light in front of it, something materially valuable was inside. Then too, they were hungry. So we told them: "Listen, we don't want you to tamper with the box. It is very special to us and we believe, as Catholics when Jesus held the bread at His last supper and said: 'Take this (the bread,) all of you and eat it for this is my body. Do this in remembrance of Me.' – He really meant what He said." We explained: "To you it would look only like a tiny piece of bread, but to us the real presence of the bodily Christ is there. That is why it is so special." They both looked down at their feet and didn't utter a word.

Then we told them: "If you are hungry when you come down into the holler and want something to eat, just take it from the refrigerator or cupboards but...please leave us a note that you were here and took food." It wasn't long afterward, we came home one day to see a note swinging on the pull string from the kitchen light bulb. It said: "We were here and took some oranges, peanut butter and crackers." Jane and I smiled. That tactic worked and we had them as friends for many years.

So besides the work or ministry that we did in the county folks came across the threshold of our life in the holler. Many needed assistance of some kind, whether it was a helping hand or a listening heart. Oftentimes, we were the ones needing a hand to get out of a ditch, fix a flat, jump a dead battery or repair a roof.

Tom, great carpenter that he was, assisted us in building a barn, a chapel in the woods, and two hermitages over the space of several years. I was able to leave the house and reside in one of the cabins in the woods – getting back to having hours alone in solitude. O what a joy it was! Jane had a much bigger bedroom in the main house now that the partition was down. We had a worship space, deep in the woods; a rustic chapel where we could meditate and pray the Office. One hermitage was used for guests, those folks who wanted to get away for awhile from the hectic pace of city life and find some time to spend with God in silence.

CHAPTER 10

The County and the County Seat

"While with an eye made quiet by the power of harmony, and the
deep power of joy, we see into the life of things." (William Wordsworth)

In Chicago if you want to tell someone where you live you
would do it in blocks – for example: 2400N meaning 24
blocks north of Downtown and 900W meaning 9 blocks
west of Lake Michigan. In WV if you ask where a person
dwells you'll most likely be told the county. There are fifty-
five of them. The town of Spencer is the seat of Roane
County WV and the center of most municipal services.

In those earlier years, the seventies, several societal
currents flowed through the county seat that seemed diametrically opposed to fusion. There were the "respectful"
town folks, the lawyers, bankers, local government officials,
doctors, teachers, and other professionals. On another
strata were the local blue collar workers, who had their
differences with the "hippies" some of whom had moved
in from outside the state to occupy a tract of land that
branched off Steel Hollow road on the outskirts of the city.
These were an eclectic, educated bunch that fled suburbia

and the middle class life-style of other states. Their community title was: "The No Names." This designation was applied because with all the different spiritualities and philosophies in the group they could not come up with one that identified them as a whole.

I loved to communicate with this group, if only because they were so different and interesting. These folks challenged their fore-bearers' lifestyle and immersed themselves in the "back-to-the-land" movement of that era. They grew their own produce, inhabited barn-like buildings, heated with wood, and lacked the amenities of electric and running water, by choice. The common clothing included baggy shirts and pants or loose, flowing flowered skirts, mud boots to the knees bandanas and beads. The guys were not clean shaven. Their hair was most often disheveled, if not in a pony tail and their bodies frequently emitted a pungent malodor – much to the chagrin of the respectable folks. The No Names believed in living simply so others could simply live. Their lifestyle was very frugal with a deep respect for the earth and its nurturance. They extended helping hands to the neighbors in the countryside around them; oftentimes for no pay. The nine to five weekly work schedule was not for them. Their priorities were relationships, even extra marital ones and this caused ambivalent feelings among the local people. The hippies were admired and loved for their gestures of outreach and helpfulness but scorned for their unkempt ways and conjugal infidelities.

They hitch-hiked, walked or biked to town and made their presence felt mostly at the Spring Creek Soy Dairy or at the Growing Tree which was the local natural food co-op. The No Names were not into much organization or book keeping so the business venture of running the store floundered continuously. However, the Growing Tree, while it lasted, was the place for friendly conversations and learning all the "alternative" news. Jane and I took pleasure and delight in sharing with people whose visions of peace, justice, and the global environs meshed with our own and extended well beyond the confines of Roane County.

There was a bulletin board plastered with notes. Examples of entries would be…"Looking to house sit for the winter; will do manual labor in exchange." Or, "I'm willing to bale hay in exchange for food." Or, "Wanted to trade: wheelbarrow for axe and maul."

One October day, close to Halloween, Stan, the tender at the store, with a background in Judaism, blundered. A friend of Sister Jane's was visiting. He was a Greek Orthodox priest, who pulled into our holler in an old station wagon with his wife and four kids. Six foot tall Father Gregory was dressed in his whole orthodox regalia of black flowing robes, tall black headdress and large pectoral cross. He went into the Growing Tree Country Store to check it out and to buy some bulk items. Stan took one look at him and exclaimed in wonderment: "Wow! What a Halloween costume!"

Not funny. However, Father Gregory told us of the episode, tongue in cheek, when he got back and we laughed heartily at his story.

Another study in contrast in our town was the Spencer State Hospital. Not long before my arrival, I was told, a train hauling many psychiatrically ill people used to arrive periodically at a tiny railroad depot near town and these folks were quickly shuttled to the facility just on the outskirts of the city. At one time there were thousands of people housed in that institution.

In Pittsburgh, Pennsylvania I had studied nursing at St. Francis Hospital, a place that was in the forefront of psychiatric treatment and evaluation in those days. There were twelve floors of patients, all separated according to their type of illness and living in relatively comfortable surroundings. The floors were carpeted. They had private rooms, decent food and cheerful recreational areas. Each section had its own nurses and aides. Psychiatrists were available and assigned to every individual.

Coming to West Virginia and witnessing Spencer State Hospital in the seventies was like being transported back in time to the 18th century. Between the floors there were spiraling, caged in, cement ramps where patients were herded (for want of a better word), from place to place. Some rooms termed: "isolation" had a twelve inch square window with metal grating in a steel door. That was the only opening to a cell with nothing in it but a naked, ranting patient and a bare single mattress on the marble floor.

While most of the patients had profound mental illness we found out that some families had put their relatives in what I'd call a "hell hole" for some lame excuse. Were they grouped according to illness? No! Oftentimes they were separated according to the county they came from! Many were "thorazined" to stupefaction; their tongues so thick they would barely move. All day long you could witness them sitting like mummies up against a dismal corridor wall, except for the ten minute smoking breaks, when, the designated room reeked with billowing plumes of grey smog that settled on everything and everyone around.

Jane and I began going there once a week to help feed lunches on the medical unit which housed folks who were both physically and mentally ill. As we worked with them how vividly the words of St. Francis in his Testament came to mind: "This is how God inspired me, Brother Francis, to embark upon a life of penance. When I was in sin, the sight of lepers nauseated me beyond measure; but then God himself led me into their company, and I had pity on them. When I had once become acquainted with them, what had previously nauseated me became a source of spiritual and physical consolation for me. After that I did not wait long before leaving the world."

Early in my novitiate days, I had learned about three forms of love. The Greeks had words for each kind; Eros: the erotic sexual love, Philia: brotherly/sisterly love, and Agape: a spiritual and selfless love. It was the last of these that played out in the interaction between Francis and the leper and between us and our friends at the state hospital. After spending time caring for these inmates we began to love them and to know beyond a doubt that each person, no matter how feeble in body, mind or spirit is unique and precious in whatever gifts they have. Each one had good qualities, even if they were buried beneath an often rough exterior. We learned that where we took love, we found love and you could never tell when it would come bursting forth disguised in a firm handshake, a wide grin or a deeply felt word of gratitude.

In the 1980's a new administrator came to the hospital and things began to change – no more solitary confinement, or drugged stupefaction. Patients were freer to be themselves and sometimes that led to more speaking out and acting out, resulting in more personnel injuries. By 1989 the huge mental institution shut its doors and patients were sent to alternative housing units or to facilities in other towns. The bulwark of monolithic proportions was bulldozed to the ground. Jane and I felt like an era had ended and we missed our friends.

In the town of Spencer there were a number of churches of all kinds of denominations. Baptists and Methodists outnumbered the others. A person had to drive the country roads to find the many smaller Pentecostal, Holiness denominations. Catholics were and still are a minority in these parts and we are often not even considered a Christian denomination. It is hard to dispel some of the myths that were entrenched here hundreds of years ago. Folks still carry within the realm of their convictions that we are papists and worshipers of the Blessed Virgin Mary.

Once in a snowstorm, Bishop Michaels drove three hours from Wheeling, West Virginia to Spencer. As the main celebrant he was due in for a Confirmation Ceremony. He got stranded at the bottom of a steep hill in a snow bank below the church. On calling our only wrecker service he was told he would have to wait as he was number fifty on the list of those needing help and they'd be with him as soon as possible. No preferential treatment for clergy around here. He was just one of the folks in need and needless to say there was no Confirmation service that night.

One of our doctors told me a story. As mentioned previously, Dr. Pedro Ambrosio and his wife Dr. Erlinda are from the Philippines. Both are dark skinned and Catholic. They came from a hectic medical practice in Harlem. NY. One day Dr. Pedro shared with me: "We were nearly shunned when first setting up practice in our community about a generation ago." That was until he saved the life of a heart attack victim who was a prominent person in the town. Then there was a marked change in some persons' attitudes. When the couple retired a few years back it was to highest accolades and praise. A new walk around the hospital was named especially for them.

The gala event that brings the whole county together and summons sons and daughters home from other states is the Black Walnut Festival during the second long weekend in October. It's prepared for a year in advance and named after the beautiful dark wood and the white meat nut trees that flourish here. There are numerous floats, marching bands, the children's parade, the crowning of the Queen of the Festival and the selection of her court. For eats, among other things, there are black walnut cakes, cookies, fudge, ox roast sandwiches and elephant ears. Biscuits and gravy, beans and cornbread are staples to it all. Square dancing in the street and live bands set the city pavement vibrating with life. The library is decked in handmade quilts and artisans booths are all around the town square. The camaraderie among the folks warms the chilly October days and helps us come together in joy before the long somber days of November and winter settle over the dark, dreary, frozen earth.

Roane County is one of the largest in the state and that has a major impact on your life if you happen to be in the police force, or on the EMS team or a Home Health nurse, or sick. I once had a patient at the southern tip of the county, down by Cottontree tell me: "We take the law into our own hands down here. Why by the time any law officer would get to these parts to settle a dispute we could all be dead!"

I guess that helps explain why in the back hills so many people have a loaded gun behind their front door. They are not mean or wicked people. They just don't want, "messed with," as they say. Protecting their own lives, their families and their property from intruders are all part of the activities of daily living.

Once I was going out over a hill off of Route 36 South. I took a right on a one lane road they call Vineyard Ridge and drove a few miles coming across a crossroad dipping down in four different directions. There were no road signs and no people around. I knew each ribbon of pavement would take me to a far opposite corner of the county and I was at a loss to know how to get to my home health patient. I waited and waited. Finally a car came along and I flagged it down only to find out it was a school teacher who did not know where on earth she was either. No cell phones then, we had to retrace our steps and start over.

As for our EMS it was easy to imagine an exasperated ambulance driver throwing his hands up in dismay when told: "Mrs. Fluharty is having a heart attack and to locate her they have to drive thirty-five miles south, take the first road off to the left down Groundhog Slide, go past a sharp bend to the right, see a huge hickory tree, a row of four mailboxes, turn right and her house is on the left." She could have been defunct and buried by the time they got there. It was all a part of life in rural Roane Co. WV. We now have 911 services – having had our fill of fatalities, and frustrated emergency personnel and home health nurses. Most of the roads presently have names and the mailboxes are numbered - Great progress.

CHAPTER **11**

Keeping Company with Mountain Spirits

"I had three chairs in my house, one for solitude,
one for company and one for society." (Walden, by H.D. Thoreau)

St. Francis always taught his followers to associate with the poor and the lowly, the Anawim. That was a term used in the Hebrew Scripture to designate people who were marginalized or oppressed, the little ones who knew their dependence on a loving God. Francis, in setting an example, could be found down in the leper colony on the outskirts of the city of Assisi bathing wounds and bandaging sores while dressed in tattered clothing and shivering from the cold himself. He identified with these cast offs of his day and it was my desire to catch a glimpse of what it was that made him so happy in this ministry.

Maybe in the poor, Francis caught the gaze of God. Maybe they had nothing of material wealth, or societal status. Perhaps some of them had interiorly, pearls of great price and that is why he loved their company.

Early in the 1980's the local health department was searching for a nurse to go out and take care of the ill in their homes, not only in the town of Spencer, but for the furthermost outreaches of our vast county. Then it was listed as a part-time job. I decided to apply in hopes of leaving the more structured, and sometimes frenetic pace of the hospital for my first love, the more hands on care and health teaching of the homebound. I deeply desired to nurse the poor of the hills and hollers in their own residences because there I realized I could really get to know them as they are in their usual environment and not the sterile atmosphere of a medical institution. The job was mine without a hassle. I doubt if they had another willing applicant.

It was a "fur piece" down to Cottontree. Many home health patients were tucked away in obscurity. One morning I was sent from our office, by her physician, to care for Mrs. Minnie Kessinger. My job was to see how she was doing and check if her medications were being taken accurately. Forty-five minutes later, with many a one lane road, winding miles, and a couple of low water crossings behind me, I found the dirt driveway leading to her single wide trailer. It was perched on a narrow strip of mountainside. To the left of her home towered a huge, moribund tree, precariously teetering over her dwelling place. All around Minnie's domain flower pots held seedlings and plants, rosebushes, begonias and all manner of green vegetation. Garden tools and paraphernalia decked out the front porch: shovel, hoe, rake, buckets, planters etc. As I was about to step across the threshold dogs began to bark excitedly on the other side of the trailer door. A few moments after I knocked, she appeared with the two little yipping canines. Minnie was a wee mite of a thing with a heavy robe, thick, wooly knee socks, and a toboggan on her head. It didn't matter how hot it got Minnie let me know she always wore a cap to keep from catching a cold.

After explaining who I was and why her doctor had sent me, a wide, welcoming smile spread across her gentle, cross-hatched, wrinkled face. "Well come on in," Minnie said, as she beckoned me toward a heavily stuffed couch, covered with a throw on account of the dogs. "Have yourself a seat." She motioned toward the sofa as the two highly wired critters, circling furiously around my ankles, clamored for attention, and got it. Minnie assured me: "They won't bite you. Don't worry." It took a lot of trust to believe her. I reached down to pet them and whisper sweet nothings. Eventually they settled down...on my lap.

My job was to get a health history, take vital signs: blood pressure, temperature, respirations and pulse. Health visits always required a physical assessment, progress notes, and medication compliance. Health teaching comprised instruction about the current illness, disease process, effectiveness of medicines and so forth.

As I pulled the blood pressure apparatus out of my bag, I noticed that Minnie's place was well cared for. Lacy white curtains dipped in folds across the lengthy living room window. A few of her home-made crafts, works in progress, lay on a nearby dining room table. An old wide screen TV kept her in touch with the world outside.

When I launched into questions about her health history, I got more history than I had bargained for. I let Minnie talk on for awhile because I knew it was good for the nurse-patient relationship, but also because I was fascinated by her story. She stole my heart away as she shared about her undying love for her children, her persistence, her faith and her courage in the midst of a horrendous deck of ill-fated life circumstances.

One circumstance was 'a poundin.' She expounded: "They had me a poundin."

"What is that?" I questioned her. She replied as her eyes glistened moist.

"My alcoholic husband stole a family's car, which happened to belong to the foreman of the local coal mine. Then he took what was left of the script for the groceries in the county store. drank down on it and left."

He left Minnie with two small children to care for on her own. Elaborating on the incident, she proceeded: "I had a letter [meaning she was a bona fide member], in the Straight Creek Baptist Church. The foreman and his family belonged there too. One evening I went to the church and they sent me home. I thought it was because my husband stole the foreman's car, and I cried." Later that evening they came and laid boxes of groceries on my back porch. That's a poundin'.

Another day when I went to see her I said: "Minnie, tell me a bit about your own family background." She began: "I was born on January 2, 1920 in Sevire County, Tennessee of an Irish father, James Christopher, and I had a Cherokee Indian mother, Alice Spurgeon. I was the last of eight siblings: Lillard, Lula, Willie, Elmer, Perl, Walter and Ruth. My dad was first a farmer but then the family moved to coal mining country in Kentucky when I was two years old. Dad worked the mines and drank. We moved from coal camp to coal camp till I was nine years old. We walked a mile to school." Divulging secrets of those days, she continued: "Oftentimes we'd wear women's stockings with the feet cut off and the ends tucked under. Other kids

KEEPING COMPANY WITH MOUNTAIN SPIRITS ✔

had peanut butter crackers in their lunches. We had only pone dog bread and fatback bacon. I had to quit school at eighth grade because I had no decent clothes or money for books. It broke my heart."

Reminiscing for a moment I thought of my own childhood when I complained about having to clean eggs for sale and work in the garden with the produce but, we certainly had socks, shoes, and boots. We didn't think peanut butter sandwiches were rich fare in our packed lunches. As for not graduating from high school – that question would not have even entered our minds.

As I stood and went over to the sink to get her a glass of water, Minnie's tale clipped on at a fast pace: "Meanwhile with my dad drinking, mom had to work taking in the 'awefullest' filthy washings and she did them on a scrub board after carrying water from a neighbor's house. My mom died when she was seventy-nine because her body and her heart wore out and she got to fallin'. She was a good Christian. We had her laid out in a nylon dress with eleven yards of lace and a built up slip."

"What is a built up slip?" I asked. She replied:

"I made the skirt of the dress with all that yardage of lace and I attached a slip underneath it."

"Bet it was simply beautiful!" I responded. Minnie smiled quietly and nodded.

Another time when we got to talking – which by now took no effort at all- I asked about her father: "Whatever happened to him Minnie?" Without blinking an eye she replied:

"He died in a coal mine. They would dynamite a mine; then the cars would come along and go into the rooms and pick up the coal. My dad was waiting for the first car, but the car got away from the motorman and bumped my father up against the face of the coal and cut him in two." I swallowed hard and sickened at the thought of it. However, it seemed to me that Minnie and her mom had seen so many dreadful experiences at the hand of her dad that she was not devastated by his untimely, gruesome death.

She went on with the history: "I married young, and by age twenty I had two children. With my second pregnancy I was anemic. The doctor gave me a Vitamin B - 12 shot and told me to rest, and to gain all the weight I could. I was poor as a snake. I guess the shots made Larry [her son], lay so low down. You shoulda' seen my feet and legs swelled. I had him regular [natural childbirth], at home. It was in October around the time of the World Series. Both father and son were doctors. The son came first and because I was in hard labor pains he gave me a 'twilight capsule' and went to take care of another woman." As an aside Minnie interjected: "I wouldn't have him for a cat havin' kittens." That is how much she came to value his skills. She went on: "Then the older doctor, his father, came in and he was mad." He said:

"When you do something like that; [giving a twilight capsule which slowed down the labor pains,] you might as well put a woman in a room, lock the door, throw the key away, and go leave her." Then he grabbed a magazine and sat down.

"They didn't take babies then." Minnie told me. "They knew nothin' about C-sections. Larry was broad shoulders, and his head came out in two pains. The doctor cut me. The baby wasn't breathing. He told the midwife to get cold water. He should have known there was no refrigeration in the coal camps except for the wealthy. She went and got some and put me and Larry in a chill. Larry weighed over thirteen pounds. We both survived." She continued on: "I had a hysterectomy at twenty-one and that put me into push menopause." (By push menopause I learned she meant that menopause came early due to the hormone alterations after the hysterectomy.) I surmised the doctors didn't want any more thirteen pound babies coming out of a ninety-nine pound mother.

Her husband's drinking continued. She and her children were never assured of what she called; "another meal ahead or being set out on the road." One day when he was in jail Minnie told me: "I sat down on the back steps. I didn't know what to do. I believe it was the lowest I'd ever been in my life. I prayed: 'Lord there's three of your children down here (meaning herself and the two little ones), that needs You and my back is against the wall. If You'll help me to make a way and help me to get a job and get to Charleston, West Virginia, You'll never find me sitting like this again.' And you know that was the last of September and by the following January I took the kids out of the school in Boone County, Kentucky on Friday evening and on Monday morning put them in school in Charleston. I went all over the city looking for a job, except in bars, and soon found one in a cleaning establishment."

Her first husband died in 1987 from a heart attack. She told me: "When he was on his way to the hospital for the last time he was praying but he didn't make it." Minnie married Archie Kessinger in 1956 and lived happily with him till his demise of a heart attack in 1980.

In living out her senior years alone Minnie keeps busy with her crafts and her green thumb. I enjoyed and learned from her witticism and her wit. One day she asked: "Do you deal in flowers?" She was inquiring whether or not I liked flowers. After my nod of affirmation, she continued: "I've been flowerin'." She had been potting plants and planting seeds that morning. She confided to me that she learned her love of flowers from her Uncle Bruce and Aunt Tish. Reminiscing, she went on: "We'd talk to them, cry over them, baby them and they'd bloom."

As I made a visit one fall day she quipped: "I held you in honor of a few dahlia bulbs. These are for you." Later she gave me an in-service regarding the holin' of apples, potatoes, and pears to keep them till spring. Holin' is a term Minnie used for preserving fruit or potatoes through the winter without the benefit of refrigeration. "You dig trenches, put barrels in them, cover them over with dirt,

KEEPING COMPANY WITH MOUNTAIN SPIRITS ❧

except at one end, line them with leaves, put in the pro-duce and bank them in the front with sawdust."

Each time I would visit Minnie she seemed to come up with a new twist of a phrase I hadn't heard before and I did often wonder where some of the expressions origi-nated. One time she said: "I'm awful greedy." That meant that she was very hungry. On another occasion she spoke about her escapades to the second hand stores which she dubbed: "dig and paw places."

During one instance I remember telling her about my friend who was a potter and how she fired her pots in an electric kiln. Minnie told me of an acquaintance of hers who did that kind of work in Tennessee. She said: "He has a brick oven that he kills his stuff in."

One time she was explaining about having a hard night. Her face looked a bit more tired and drawn. I asked her what was wrong. She said: "I had the Black Flux." That term was not to be found in any nursing books or journals I had read. No teacher ever taught us about such a condi-tion. After trying to figure it out I finally gave up and asked: "Minnie, just what is the Black Flux?" She said:

"You know; the diarrhear!"

Months after this incident, I happened to read a biog-raphy of St. Thomas More, an Englishman and lawyer, who gave up his life for his beliefs at the time of King Henry VIII. To my astonishment, there was a plague around that time and people died of the Black Flux! I had to wonder, how many of Minnie's phrases had their roots in Old English?

Now approaching ninety Minnie, my mountain mama friend, still shines with a bright spirit that seems to perme-ate every cell of her tiny frame. She is not so wise in book learning but she is a veritable storehouse of insights on life journeying. She has a simple faith and trust in God that has deepened with her own experience of much suffering. I would call her a wisdom figure in my life and a companion for my own sojourn, because, despite all her misfortunes and setbacks she has triumphed with an indomitable spirit of quiet joy, lightsomeness of heart and deep confidence in her Father's care. If anyone personified the spirit of the Anawim in my life it was Minnie. The gentle perfume of her life wafted across the mountains, like the lilies of the valley that grace our earthen floors.

Another woman with a spunky soul was Vada Swiney. Vada taught me tenacity of spirit. She inhabited a tiny, one story, two room, red, fake-brick house in Walton. Walton was only a half hour drive away from the nursing office. It was the entrance to her house that proved a challenge. On a rainy day only a dope would dare to go up the slick, slimy, red clay incline in a jeep for fear of skidding over the ravine backwards. I had attempted it. A nearby neighbor, upon seeing my endeavor from his front porch screeched out: "Don't you know any better than to try to get up that mountain when it's wet?!" In rainy or snowy conditions, any visitor, nurse or otherwise had to walk in from the other end of the property, down a hill, across a rickety wooden bridge (that was minus a few slats), over a gurgling stream, through a meadow, and up the hill to her back door.

My first greetings then were from the, too numerous to mention, cats and kittens scampering from under the house. The dog a Terrier dubbed Sparky, gleefully hyped up on chocolate candy bars came next, then finally Vada ambled to the door, with her four legged walker, delighted as ever to have a visitor that wasn't a menace. She was dressed in a white and black checkered dress that flowed gently over her portly frame. A bandana was tied securely over her head and into a knot at the nape of her neck, while a few stray curls squirmed out from beneath it to frame her ruddy skinned, high cheek-boned face.

Before she ushered me through the back door and into her house she had to show me her garden. Though she could barely walk that did not stop her from putting in a few tomatoes, pole beans, cucumbers, and other greens in her patch. She would simply sit down on a low standing bench, take it slow, and inch along the rows. She was determined. I wondered how many young folks today would be so persistent when faced with such odds. To top off the difficulty of the garden venture she had to manipulate a bailer to get water. Nearby the garden was her well. Once I saw the effort she made to get some water it was easy to understand why cleanliness was not on the top list of priorities. Like mine, it was a cylindrical well. However, hers had a slightly bent casing through which she let the bailer down. This made it difficult to obtain the water which was a precious commodity and not to be disposed of lightly.

Vada spent nearly all of her days alone and some of her nights were fear-filled. I asked once if she had any problems with neighbors who lived up the holler. She replied: "Yes." Then she took me to the screen door in the back of the house and exclaimed: "I know how to get rid of people when they come down off that mountain in the evening and attempt to do me harm." She reached for the can of Raid Insect Repellant. Holding the nozzle near the door frame she demonstrated: "I squirt this in their face, in the dark and psssssssst they're gone!" It is a mountain mama's form of tear gas."

There were days when I visited her that I was stifled by

the heat of her unvented gas stoves. I saw so many of them in the county and they were not safe but it was impossible to try and get some people to change their heating preferences. Most of the folks grew up with wood stoves and now, in their old age, there was just too much hard work connected with this means of heat to be practical. The old folks would turn the gas space heaters on full blast, without a window open anywhere. It was enough to addle the wits. One time Vada related that she had seen a ten-foot tall rabbit outside her house (the story made the county paper too). I could not help but wonder if the fumes had not befuddled her mind. She could be so funny.

During another nursing visit I sat at the bedside to take her blood pressure and a blood sample to test her sugar. She utterly surprised me by saying: "I love you because you are not afraid to touch me." Tears came to my eyes. I thought of St. Francis and the leper colony, where, as in the time of Christ they had to cry out: "Unclean! Unclean!" No one was allowed to come near them for fear of being contaminated by the dreaded Hansen's Disease. Francis and his followers did. People get ostracized because they are different. Vada was truly loveable and huggable to me. She was not someone to be afraid of. She would have given me anything in her house had I needed it. We shared many an expresso-like cup of coffee together. Once she sent me off demanding that I take a bag of her frozen strawberries. Who will ever know the depths of loneliness she experienced, or the isolation she must have felt after her beloved husband had passed away a few years earlier. Vada lived in unwanted solitude ever since. Edgar had gotten weaker and weaker and had made several trips to the hospital. As the end of his earthly life approached, I think his wife had a transforming experience herself. She looked at me one day and shared some of the moments surrounding his death. This loving widow told me in hushed tones: "Just before he died - his face was so beautiful when God came in." She had done her best to care for him over a lengthy illness. They were a childless couple except for the fact that they had taken one lad in and raised him – a person I never met and whom she rarely saw. He did not live anywhere nearby. Scarce were the folks who ever climbed the mountain to spend time with her.

In perusing spiritual books and from the advice of a spiritual director, I learned that oftentimes when God wants to draw someone close to Himself he takes away their friends and companions so that they really have to rely on Him. I think that is what happened to Vada. For all the loneliness in her life she was not a person turned in on herself. She knew where her life and strength came from and she witnessed that to me, powerfully.

Sometimes in my travels I'd be introduced to folks living by themselves but not necessarily needing any in home health care. One of them was Columbia Drake. She was commonly known as "Lummie," and it was my joy to be in her company. She was near eighty years of age, and resided in a small one floor, tar papered, green bungalow next to a Columbia Gas operation field down on Route 36. Lummie was a lesson for me in womanly moral strength and ingenuity. Silky, long white hair encased her rotund face with its flashing eyes and ready smile. She reigned from her double bed. There was a queen-like air about her. Propped up with pillows to a sitting position, she ruled from that vantage point; encircled by her food, books, writing materials, telephone, clock, and other things necessary for daily living. Every morning a worker came in about 8:00 am to help with Lummie's personal hygiene, cook breakfast, and set up the crock pot with the rest of the days' main food. After noon Lummie was alone except for the visitors or mailman or whoever else entered her home where the door was never locked.

On one occasion I asked: "What made you bedfast?" She told me her story of what she called "childbed fever." That was a condition I had heard about long ago in nursing school, called Puerperal Infection. When she was a young pregnant woman and about to deliver the doctors went around on horses delivering babies one after another. Aseptic technique or measures to prevent the spread of disease were not required or even known. They would leave one delivery, head on to the next and never even wash their hands, let alone don gloves.

Shortly after Lummie gave birth to her child a horrendous infection set up in her abdomen and she told me: "I nearly died. The fever went so high I had to be taken, in the winter, on a sled for miles to the main road and then on to the hospital in Charleston. The infection set in so deep it near destroyed the bones in my hips and finally over the years they just gave out."

As we were sharing one day I said: "Lummie, you are all alone here, what if someone would come through that front door and try to hurt you?" She looked at me rather sheepishly and replied matter-of-factly: "You see that over there?" Her gaze landed on a rifle by her bed. I swallowed hard and said: "Yes." She set her piercing eyes on me and whispered:

"I'd ventilate em." No spineless mountain mama here, I thought. That was Lummie. She would act in self-defense but to all others that crossed her threshold she was a ray of sunshine, possessed by a love, which listened attentively and treated everyone with tenderness.

These are qualities which seemed to be common traits among so many of the women in this county. They have remained steadfast through countless privations and hardships. Their spirits are dauntless and courageous even in the face of death. There is an inner wisdom that intuitively knows what true values are and how to uphold them. And finally, they seem to have an innate compassion for all created things and people that suffer because they too have suffered and they know the journey.

There is a book called the Fioretti (Little Flowers of St. Francis,) and it contains many colorful vignettes in the lives of the early Franciscan Friars portraying their humble simplicity. One story is told of a Brother Juniper and the sick brother who was sure he would get well if only he could eat a roasted pig's foot. Juniper, thinking that he simply had to meet the need went and cut off a foot of a nearby farmer's pig, much to the anger and consternation of the farmer. Juniper's simplicity reminded me of the day Scotty, a neighbor came, full of angst to my place, worried not about a pig but about his heifer.

It was an early spring morning and a gentle overnight shower accentuated the myriad shades of new green leaves on the trees around the hermitage. As I went about my usual morning chores of bailing up the water, banking the wood stove and getting breakfast ready, the warbling of the birds in the Rose of Sharon bush outside the kitchen window rose in pitch, swelled in volume and almost drowned out the rapid knocking sound on the front door.

Scotty stood on the threshold of the century-old porch,

his ruddy, high cheek-boned Cherokee face, and deep-set eyes now shrouded in anxiety. Scotty was my nearest neighbor who lived with his wife, Ruth, half a mile away up on the ridge. He had on his bib overalls, old long sleeved shirt and "mudders." (These are boots all of one piece that came up as far as the knees). He had trekked all the way down the hill to fetch me.

He spurted out: "I'm worried and I know something bad has happened:" Scotty had a warm and tender love for all creatures, and more especially his cows. This particular morning his one pregnant heifer was missing - hadn't been home all night. He asked if I wouldn't come with him right away.

I had learned to listen to the intuitions of these hill folks. So off we went, rain gear, knee high boots and all, over the hills, through the briars, and multi-flora rosebushes. Now typically, pregnant cows will go to the outposts of the property against the farthest fence line, and completely out of view to drop their newborns. Sure enough, at the east-ern-most end by the barbed-wire fence, there was Scotty's heifer, prostrate on the ground, legs stretched out rigid, her neck arched and eyeballs rolling back in her head. The cow's udder was flaming red, swollen and hot. Not one drop of milk was going to come from those tits. The little black calf needing that precious liquid was only a few feet away, moaning pitifully.

"Go to Southern States (a country Co-op), and get some (what at least sounded like), Cal de Mag and bring it back here. Quick!" Scotty ordered.

Back through the woods, up to the hilltop, out over the ridge and down to the town of Spencer I went, gunning the old Chevy as fast as I dared. Southern States was one of those stores where a person could find almost anything needed for life in the country. I explained our predicament. Here, the sales folks were informed and eager to share their knowledge with the farmers. Forty-five minutes later I was back, holding an enema-bag-like contraption filled with a solution, and connected to a long tube with a wide-bore needle at the end. I shuddered to think of what the next step might be in our attempt to get the heifer on her feet. I was eyeing the long needle when Scotty said: "Okay, stick it in the cow." To which I replied:

"What? I never stuck a cow before. I'm a nurse, not a veterinarian!"

"A nurse'll do fine." He answered. I knew there was no right way out of the situation. I thought: St. Francis should see this. Maybe he did.

"Scotty, where's the alcohol?" I asked.

"You don't need to rub a cow with alcohol." He responded. Now, I had given injections to many humans, but despite Scotty's confidence in me, a heifer just isn't the same.

"Where do I put the shot, Scotty?" He pointed to the posterior.

"Oh Lord!" I muttered. Little had I realized what God would ask for when I left an inner-city ministry in Chicago for a life close to the country folks in Appalachia.

With one strong plunge, the needle penetrated the cowhide and sank into the muscle. The cow didn't flinch but, she didn't get better either. An hour later, she was definitely worse. Her eyes were further back in her head. She was lying on the ground in a posture of sheer prostration. The bladder bag was red and hotter and the teats were tightly closed.

More mandates tumbled out of Scotty's mouth: "Go call Doc Porter and see if he's home. Tell him what's going on and ask if'n he'll come."

So once again over the hills and through the thickets to find Dr. Porter I went. A telephone call and an hour later, here he came with his bag and his bicycle tire pump. I was beginning to wonder about veterinary practices in the state. "What's the pump for?" I asked. He looked at me as if to infer: Just you wait and see.

We no sooner got to the site of the trauma and Doc inserted the pump nozzle gently inside a tit and gave the pump handle one good push. I couldn't believe my eyes: air up and in, pressure released at the opening, and then warm milk gushing out! The other three teats got the same procedure with the same results. Soon, the udder bag resumed its normal pink color. Mama heifer struggled to her feet. The newborn calf suckled successfully and finally, the happy duo followed us back through the woods to the meadow. When we parted that afternoon, the smile on Scotty's face stretched ear-to-ear: he was so grateful you'd have thought we'd saved his own mother.

At the top of one of the nearby ridges lived a freckled faced, impish-grinned kid named Huck. He was a boy who could never pass a pop machine without checking the drop tray for any forgotten change. "Optimism" should have been his middle name. He dwelt in a tar-papered house supported at one end on a high stack of un-cemented, cement blocks. The front screen door swung eerily at night on one hinge and the drafty old place welcomed every shaft of cold air that wafted across the mountains. Inside the fragile homestead Stacey, his mom, and four other siblings struggled daily to survive on this planet earth. Stacey had experienced a disadvantaged, abusive childhood and so as soon as possible she escaped her family home to couple up with a man who had no intention of being a supportive husband and loving father. The scene repeated itself several times with the result that Stacey had a house full of children to cherish with a mother's care. She loved them deeply and did her best to provide for them. Never once did the fathers cross the threshold to lend a helping hand or a listening heart.

One fall season when Huck was in fifth grade it was decided that the class would take a bus trip to the nation's capitol. Long in advance, car washes and bake sales preceded the event in order to pay for the bus fare, meals and a night's lodging. The eagerly anticipated moment arrived and the class with their teacher boarded the Greyhound bound for D.C. All his other classmates had some spending money, but not Huck. The teacher, loving person that she was, slipped him a twenty on the sly and off they went to see the sights. With awe and pride they viewed the nation's capitol, the national monuments the White House, the Smithsonian Institute and the other buildings so totally foreign looking to their county's structures. The students delighted in learning so much about our country's history. As they walked along the side-walks that cold, frosty November morning Huck spied a huge cardboard box, like one that would hold a large appliance such as a washer. Inquisitive as always he had to lift the lid and peek inside. A flabbergasted expression crossed his face. Down at the bottom of the box was a young woman with a tiny infant huddled against the cold, peering up at him. Huck stammered: "Where is your home?" She replied:

"We don't have a home." With that Huck thrust his hand down into his jeans pocket, grasped the twenty-dollar bill and insisted that the woman take it. At first she declined but then in her need she accepted it with a kind smile and a heart full of gratitude.

A few paces away a tear rolled down his teacher's cheek as she witnessed this display of total generosity – a gift given totally and freely by one who had no more left for himself. Then she reached down into her bag and grasped another twenty for the moment when Huck would slip past her again.

When I first learned of this story I could not help but think of Huck's mom. For all her so-called "failures" in life she certainly righted many of them in this son of hers who so spontaneously reached out in compassionate love for a mother and her child.

Billowy patches of white fluff dotted the mountainside off of Colt Ridge one morning as I drove the little Nissan truck in the direction of town. I wondered if the "fluff" were remnants of dispersing, low-lying clouds or Mr. Gandee's sheep grazing on the rocky slopes below. As I drew closer I saw that these were a different breed than the one he had before. The previous sheep were Cheviots. I came to learn that his present flock was Scottish Black Face. They had spindly legs, long staple coarse white fleece, of the stuff that is great for hand-weavers' rugs.

Denver Gandee's love for sheep goes way back to the 1930s when he was a young, bare-foot, lad in a 4 H group who cried when his pet lamb got its tail docked. That is how he began his Hall of Fame career and later spent 25 years as President of the Northwestern Livestock Marketing Association. He told me he was the first in our area to have a Merino flock and that they were introduced into America, from Spain by Thomas Jefferson. He said: "In

1900 there were 26,000 head of sheep in Roane County and the wool clip was 67,000 lbs."

Mr. Gandee didn't really care much about wool. Shepherding sheep was his passion. Now he is 85 years young and he can no longer bound the hillsides looking after them and providing for their needs.

One day I asked him why he changed breeds and got the Scottish Black Face ones. He told me these sheep were easier to care for and I wondered what he meant. How could that be? Anyone who knows about these ruminants realizes that sheep are not among God's list of most intelligent animals. They are very loveable but, very dim-witted too. In his old plaid shirt, blue jeans and aged leather boots he began to walk slowly and gingerly over the uneven terrain to the fence in his back yard while motioning for me to come with him.

We soon came to the barbed wire fence and pasture gate. There he picked up a half bucket of cracked corn and began yelling with a crackly voice: "SHEEP, SHEEP!" Before I knew what was happening, more than twenty blobs of white came bounding over the hills to his feet and the handfuls of grain he was cheerfully scattering before them. Denver, smiled, chuckled and said with delight: "I don't have to go after these sheep. They come to me. Then at night they go by instinct down there to the barn." (He pointed to a place far down on the mountain where a leaning structure of wooden boards and a tin roof clung to the hillside).

Now Mr. Gandee can no longer care for his sheep at all and he sold them to a shepherd who pastures them there right on the farm. That way Denver can still be close to the flock without the anxiety of knowing they are well cared for. One day I took him a small rug that I wove from his fleece. An expression of sheer delight lit up the old shepherd's face.

KEEPING COMPANY WITH MOUNTAIN SPIRITS ❧

It would not be hard to write a Fioretti type book here in Appalachia. Life lived close to the land, with simple, loving folks who have a predilection for taking good care of their critters are part and parcel of the stories of daily life. As I went around the county nursing the folks it seemed the farmers knew the names of all their cows, pigs, horses or goats and sheep. The animals are the next closest things to kin. To care for them tenderly seems to be in their blood. I found that when a fellow gets old, even loses his wife in death, the farm animals give him a raison d'être. Take them away and you might as well bury him. If people abuse their livestock and it's found out, the story can be in the local paper for weeks on end. The guilty parties may well find themselves with hefty penalties and a jail sentence.

The Cure of Ars, also known as St. John Vianney was a saintly parish priest in an obscure town in France in the 19th century. He once made the remark: "Salvation comes easy to country people." I think he meant that country people have a tendency to be in touch with the earth, through all the seasons; snow, rain and drought, the planting and harvesting and the birthing and dying of animals. They are in tune with creation and the Creator.

Folks of Roane County have taught me not only how to live happily but to die happily. One man, who deeply touched my life in this way, was Okey. Early on a Monday morning a distraught voice stammered over the phone line into our home health office. "Could you come quickly?" It was Jody. Her dad, Okey, was one of our patients in the end stages of congestive heart failure. We'd seen him many times before but today she reported that his legs were so swollen with fluid that they were oozing water through the pores. He was in horrific pain and having trouble breathing. Jody had given him his last available dose of morphine a few hours ago through the intravenous insertion site in his arm.

Assuring her I'd get the medication and be down as quickly as possible seemed to calm and comfort her. However, in Roane County, that "quickly" wasn't very fast. This county is one of the largest in the state topographically. Oftentimes we'd have to go thirty-five miles or more to get to a first patient on our daily list. Those miles are not a "straight stretch" as some natives call them. There are numerous blind curves. Gravel or mud rutted roads, and swinging bridges o'er swollen streams are just a few obstacles. Often a driver encounters duck, cow, and guinea chicken parades across the road at the most inopportune times. And...where the secondary roads are two lanes there is usually a solid yellow line down the center. Forget passing: passing logging trucks, or hay wagons, or garbage dumpsters or farm tractors, or the little ole' person who is leisurely surveying the countryside.

So the journey to Clio that morning took forty-five minutes. As I swung into the lane in front of the sizeable two story, gabled, farm house, all was quiet and the sky was a pale azure blue. An aura seemed to hang around the place, a sacred kind of stillness. I had a feeling that the one St. Francis called, "Sister Death," was here. Jody stood in the front doorway before I even knocked. She whispered: "He went into a coma about a half hour ago. There is no response. It doesn't even look like he is breathing and I can't feel a pulse."

Sure enough, I thought as I approached the bedside. His diaphragm was barely flickering. Pulling out the blood pressure cuff and stethoscope from my bag I tried to palpate a pulse in his arm: nothing. There was no audible blood pressure; no palpable carotid pulse either. The time for clinical skills to bow out had arrived. All Okey and Jody could benefit from now were compassion and love. I held her for a moment. There was such a strong bond of affection between Jody and her dad. She had seen him suffer so long with a worn out heart, caring for him day and night. I know it was terribly hard for her to let him go.

I asked: "Would you like to say a prayer with me for your dad?" She nodded in affirmation. She rested her hand on his shoulder and I put my hand on his arm. A son of Okey's was on the other side of the bed, while the rest of the members of the large family were speaking in hushed tones out in the kitchen. I began: "Our Father..." The three of us were totally unprepared for what happened next. Okey sat bolt upright, not saying a word but with his eyes wide open and sharply focused on something above and straight ahead of him. Jody and I looked at each other spellbound as goose bumps covered our arms and we gasped for a breath. "Should we finish the Our Father?" I hesitatingly asked. Jody nodded and we proceeded.

All the while Okey's eyes were transfixed and his arms

were flailing as if to say: "Let me out of this worn out body!" He was sitting straight up in bed, with his eyes riveted on the beyond. Knowing that hearing is the last sense to leave, I leaned over and whispered in his ear: "Okey, do you see the Lord? Do you see the Lord? GO TO HIM! GO TO HIM!"

With eyes still firmly focused ahead and above himself he heaved one last sigh, laid back on the pillow and was gone. Great peace and a sense of awe enveloped us in that moment. This experience, which happened more that sixteen years ago, is etched as clearly in my mind and heart today, as it was then. What an awesome privilege; to be present when the veil of eternity lifted and a long-suffering soul winged its way home.

Some of the most isolated and humble souls are filled with wisdom and tender love in the hills and hollers of WV. They are the ones who have taught me important messages about life. These folks are the pearls that lie hidden to the casual observer, like the violets and coltsfoot that speckle the mountain pathways to their homes.

CHAPTER **12**

Ecstasy Turned Agony

"Into each life some rain must fall. Some days must be dark and dreary."

(H.W. Longfellow)

Seventeen years elapsed as Jane and I share our lives in Colt Run Holler. In the beginning we had a rhythm of personal and communal prayer. She spent some of her working hours as a potter and teacher of what was known as a very successful, "Punkin' Patch." The "Patch" was a part-time pre-school type of program initially housed in the basement of the parish rectory. I was engaged in part-time nursing, first at the hospital and later out in the county in folks' homes. My craft was hand-loom weaving. We both maintained the grounds and little cabins around our home and we each plugged into the manual work of gardening, canning and getting in the winter wood. As folks of limited means came across our threshold we tried to help them as our resources allowed.

As time went by tension mounted between Jane and I. As much as she pressed toward extended activity I retreated more and more into deeper solitude, distancing myself from what I felt to be her extended social involvements. In addition to the pottery Jane became deeply committed to Religious Education in the parish and also headed up Roane Rural Housing (a project to help the poor in our county). She was active in peace and justice issues during the time of so much civil strife in El Salvador and Nicaragua. All the endeavors were very praiseworthy but, I craved silence and solitude. Our vision, though it had much in common also contained, as Jane would finally state: "We have two very different non-negotiable stances and we'll never come together."

It seemed to me that there was never quiet or order around our little main house anymore. The phone was always ringing for Jane. The tempo of life went from adagio to staccato.

To illustrate the difference in our personalities: Once I thought I'd do a service and while Jane was away I scrubbed down her pottery/art shop. The walls were completely spattered with clay globs and stuff was lying all around. Was that ever a mistake! When she came home, she was so incensed that I had cleaned her workplace. Okay, I learned never again to do such a thing. It was her space and it was as she wanted it; better not to tamper with an artist's domain. A lesson was absorbed.

At another time, in early fall, Jane was busy trying to get ready for a big pottery show. Her items had to be glazed, fired, labeled and packed. She was running behind and pinched for time. I was tired from doing nearly all of the chores around the homestead, cleaning house, meals, garden work etc when she said: "Would you clean my bedroom?" Something in me snapped and I think it was the long buried memory of the art shop incident. I replied emphatically: "No. I will not!" We did not part on amicable terms the next day.

In hindsight, I recognized a big blunder I had made at the beginning of the relationship when I was so eager for Jane or another person to share some community life with. I did not insist that each person had to contribute substantially to the common fund so we could meet living expenses. I took it for granted that each one would automatically see there had to be some equality of income. While Jane or others who came later were not lazy by any means; neither did their activities bring in near enough funds for our monetary needs. Added to these were a potter's expenses of clay, electric kiln etc. I felt resentful when it seemed the burden was nearly all on my shoulders and angered when checks would repeatedly bounce.

Still we doggedly pressed onward trying so hard to make our lifestyle work over so many years. We went for counseling sessions, studied the Enneagram (a Sufi type program to help us understand our motivations and behaviors better). We also undertook a four day, professionally monitored program, on the Myers-Briggs Personality Profiles, only to learn that our two personalities were almost totally incompatible! To give just a brief sketch of what the profiles teach – there are eight traits, some dominating over others that help define a person's profile. The traits are as follows: Extrovert/Introvert, iNtuitive/Sensing, Thinking/Feeling, and Judging/Perceiving. For example a person could be ENFP or INFJ, meaning that one's dominant characteristics are: extrovert, intuitive, feeling and perceiving. The other person's are introvert, intuitive, feeling and judging. The way these two individuals live and deal with life varies greatly. Jane was a high extrovert and I was a high introvert. Jane was a perceiving person and I was a judging person.

An extrovert's understanding grows as the result of on-going interaction with people, things and events. Their reflection follows action. The introvert's approach to life is deliberate and studied. With them action follows reflection.

The perceiving person likes to take a long time to develop a wider understanding of what they are thinking about and respond to events in an unhurried flexible way. The judging person, once aware of something that calls for action, or taking a position, likes to proceed in a purposeful, organized way.

One personality type is not better than the other, only different. To give a homely illustration of what I mean: We were trying to come to an important decision affecting our life together. I had dwelt long and hard on the topic at hand and then stated what I thought we should do. Jane on the other hand would come out spontaneously with something totally the opposite of my idea. I'd get flustered and she'd say to me: "Well, that's not my final word. I'm only processing."

A few other women joined us during those days of difficulties to see our lifestyle and none stayed. They sensed the strained atmosphere between Jane and me. They did ask: "What was life really about on Colt Run?" When we could not satisfactorily explain in word or deed they eventually left. Only one, at our invitation, in 1990 came to live a few hundred yards down the road from us in the small cabin I first occupied in WV. Her name was Karen Karper. Karen was interested in living a strict hermetical lifestyle for awhile and she stayed for six years, then moved away and got married. While she was here, she wrote a book entitled: Where God Begins to Be, which drew some folks toward her doorsteps and...ours.

One day about three years before the "great divide" happened and when the tension was particularly oppressive Jane said to me: "Wouldn't you think of moving away to another place? Your mother could set you up."

I felt I had been torpedoed and was caught not only in a hard rainfall but in a funnel cloud. My gut convulsed. Here in the place I had founded more than 17 years ago, for the purpose of a quiet life and solitude, she was asking me if I would leave. I thought of saying to her: "You could start a house of hospitality with the backing of your whole Franciscan, motherhouse if such was God's will." Instead, I kept quiet and held my knotted stomach.

Still we went on living together. We were at an impasse and as we grew further and further apart I spent more time alone in the hermitage, back deep in the woods, eschewing confrontation. Days dragged on with tensions climbing.

During this interim, Sister Barbara Lucas, a Franciscan sister from Philadelphia, who had long been looking for a life in solitude, and Anna Joplin, came to visit Karen after they had read her book. These two stayed in our hermitages during their visits. Barbara spent some hours talking with me and as we shared deeply she became attracted to the life as I envisioned it. She went away but we kept up correspondence over the next couple of years and I shared her letters with Jane.

Eventually and by mutual agreement, both Barbara and Anna came to live on the property here. Barbara had a prayerful, loving, lively, and generous spirit. Anna was gentle but more withdrawn and had low energy. I wondered if she would last long in the rather rugged terrain and she didn't.

Months went by and Jane initiated one of her dreams: The building of a straw bale chapel. The tensions remained but they were covered over with work and it all had Barbara wondering, whatever did she get herself into. Day followed day until one evening after supper together I spoke of making all the hermitages self-contained meaning: each one would have cooking facilities, plumbing and enough space to be able to live in them. I asked Jane if she would be willing to move out of the main house into one of the hermitages so we could use the house as a central, communal location. It was then that it seemed that Mount Vesuvius erupted in the holler. She replied:

"I am not willing to move out of the main house." I exclaimed:

"We have got to come to a decision here as to what this life is all about. Is it prayerful solitude or hospitality?" My initial vision had been to have a type of "Laura" by that is meant a communal main house surrounded by little cabins in the woods where each person would live an essentially prayerful, solitary life surrounded by nature. The main house would be used for some community meals, meetings, necessary phone conversations, laundry, processing of garden produce, and hospitality for family or occasional visitors.

Barbara and I at that time, asked for a discernment process. St. Ignatius of Loyola, the founder of the Jesuits had outlined a process to go through to help people make a wise decision about an important area of their life. This time Jane refused. I felt certain it was because we were worn out from our attempts in the past: impasse again.

One day a short while later, while Ann and Barbara were still here, I asked: "Jane, would you rather the three of us go and you stay?" She replied:

"Yes."

At my wits end, I called Father Angelus and told him what was going on and asked: "Should we leave?" At that point I was ready to pack up and exit quickly. Father said to me:

"No! You stay. Jane must go."

One morning a couple of days later, out in Fidelis Hermitage, I said to Jane: "You have to move. You need to set up our own house of hospitality and run it. You can do it. You have the gifts. I'll help anyway I can."

It was a crushing blow and the pain of it was simply agonizing, especially after all the emotional ties with friends, the loving, hard manual labor she had contributed to the place and the chapel. I felt her agony so deeply but at the same time life could just not go on the way it had. It would have been easier, I think for both of us to die than to experience the searing, excruciating pain of that moment. A life we had together and hoped for so much in the past seventeen years had crumbled. No divorce could have hurt more. And that is what it was like: a divorce, only it was between celibates, who both gave their best energies to an endeavor that was not to last, no matter how hard we had tried.

Did I have any assurance that everything would work out if Jane located somewhere else? - Not at all. We only knew that the two of us could not make it together any longer. From both of us a deeper walk in faith was demanded as we faced an uncertain future.

Soon she contacted some other Catholic sisters, who

worked with the poor on a huge isolated mountain in the West Virginia coal fields. That mount was also known as "The Knob." Many years before, a Sister Gretchen had begun a school there for the local children. Together with Sister Nancy, she lived in a dwelling that was close to a large, uninhabited wood and stone house in part of a land trust. After some negotiations with the sisters and the board of directors it was agreed that Jane could live in the vacant house rent free. It was not long before she would have an ecology center built, hold retreats, do programs and work with adults and children much to their delight.

The day was May 22, 1997 when Jane took a long walk out of our holler, carrying a clump of its earth with her to the top of Colt Ridge, and then drove away in her Subaru. She may not have known it, because of her own intense suffering, but she took a part of me too that day. The dream we had together shattered and something in both of us had died. Seventeen years before I had experienced an ecstasy of delight when she descended down the slippery path of Colt Run to dwell here and now there was an agony of pain as she pulled away.

CHAPTER 13

All the Way is the Way

"Come near me while I sing the ancient ways." W.B Yeats

Days and months have flowed into thirty-three years now and with their passing the rhythm of life has changed and become even more pensive and contemplative.

Shanti Pace Hermitage, a writer's perfect hideaway, is my favorite space. Jane is the one who named it. What that title signifies is a place of serenity where the great age-old Om sound of the universe comes to life in the silence. On a wall facing the entrance is an icon-like image of an East Indian lad, wearing only mid-thigh length shorts, as he sits in full lotus position. His jet black-haired head, shoulders, and slender arms are bent over and around a globe of the world cradled in his lap. It is a vivid reminder of a hermit's mission to intercede for our planet and those who dwell on it.

It is a joy to hike the old logging trail that winds through the woodlands above the cabin. One day I noticed a circular mound too perfectly shaped to "just have happened." I question if it is not a burial place for the "ancients." History books say that the Cherokee and Shawnee Indian tribes once roamed these parts. Pretending to put my feet in their moccasins, I count it a privilege to place footprints on their holy ground. While treading this wilderness alone it is easy to get lost in thoughts of what life must have been for them.

An untainted pristine purity in this womb of nature wraps me round. The canopy of a green cathedral; its undulating boughs and the choir of the birdsong of many winged ones surround me. White-tailed deer gracefully bound about. The squirrels incise and ingest hickory nuts, and the cool brown earth frames random seams of reddish clay beneath the feet of this happy tromping hermit.

There is an author, Benedikt Mertens ofm who explains some facets of solitude in the 11th and 12th centuries. I learned from him that hermits then did not live the same lifestyle as the ones in the early centuries of Christianity. They had different degrees of personal solitude and varying forms of community life. They frequently situated their hermitages in the wilderness of the forest or other remote areas. Essential to any hermit's life is long periods of silence and aloneness, so that one can more easily hear the voice of God. The way each person lives the solitary life may have many nuances.

For example, the Celtic hermits, like St. Kevin or St. Columba went off for months to live in a distant cave in total solitude. Then they would emerge from their hide-a-ways renewed, to go among the people to preach or teach. Some later founded monasteries that became centers of learning.

Saint Anthony of the Desert spent his whole adult life alone, living in greatest austerity and only as an old man did many gather round him magnetized by the authenticity of his teaching. St. Francis was known to spend six months of a year living in solitude. He went to a remote place for forty days at a time, as often as seven times a year. Francis would scale some steep mountain and enter a hermit's cell or cave and become absorbed in God. Then when his re-treat was over he'd take the wisdom imbibed in prayer and spill it among the people in words filled with a divine fire and a radiant joy that captivated the hearts of thousands of folks and drew many to follow him in the Gospel life.

He composed a Rule for Hermitages for his brothers that was not so strictly solitary. There were to be two "Marthas" – the active ones, and two "Marys" – the contemplative ones. The Marthas were to care for the needs of the Marys while these were given over exclusively to private prayer and the recitation of the Divine Office (the official prayer of the church, consisting mostly of psalms and scripture readings). Then the roles were to be reversed.

The person, no matter what the character of the her-metical way they choose must have a "plan of life;" at least a flexible form of a schedule. Any authentic desert father or mother would instruct their directee in this practice, so that time is not frittered away, and so the evil one would have less chance to get a hold on the unoccupied mind and spirit.

Here in the holler most days begin a 4am with quiet reflection on the readings of the liturgy of the day and commentary along with a cup of strong coffee. I find these are the best hours to sit and soak in the silence and to lis-ten to whatever the Word might be trying to tell me. Then there follows time for the morning adoration and Office, before breakfast at 7:00 am. Daily chores like getting the wood in, working in the garden, doing laundry, cleaning the cabin are done before I commence writing. At 12:00 Noon the Angelus is prayed, followed by a light lunch, a short rest, spiritual reading, and a walk. Until 4:30 pm the day's schedule varies: from working on the weaving loom, shopping for necessities, doing other manual labor, reaching out to someone in need, or just listening to someone who comes to share. In the late afternoon an hour of silent adoration before the Blessed Sacrament precedes the evening Office and reception of the Eucharist when there is no Mass. This is followed by supper and free time spent in the art shop, or reading, or exercising, and the night Office of Compline before retiring at 9:00 pm. No component of the daily routine is carved in stone because as anyone who has lived for awhile on this earth, hermit or not, knows there are always exceptions to the rule. There are some days when I sense a strong impulse of the spirit urging me to just spend time sitting at the Lord's feet, and I do. The ability to be able to rest in Him is a major delight of the hermetical life.

The Chapel of the Nativity, designed by Sister Jane in 1997 and built by a few professionals and many volunteers is a meditation space nestled here in the woods beneath black walnut trees much like the Portiuncula Chapel was secluded in the woods below the town of Assisi in St. Francis' day. Instead of being a stone structure as was the Little Portion: it is a straw bale construction. The walls are made of rectangular straw bales, held in place by metal rods. The bales are surrounded by metal chicken wire and covered with three layers of stucco. It is so air tight that nary a mouse can get in. Eight windows provide paths for shafts of light gliding over the window sills that are two feet wide (the width of a straw bale). The ample space is heated by one small propane heater making the place warm in cold weather. The width of the walls provide for less expensive heating in winter and efficient cooling in summer. A small bell tower crowns the chapel's Ondura tiled, hip roof. The doorway was constructed from aged, seasoned, oak boards by a local artist, Pete Freid. He used wooden pegs for nails and inserted a small hexagonal, emerald green and clear, beveled, stained glass window in it. The entrance way resembles an aperture common in medieval scenery or tales of Robin Hood and his merry men.

Four little hermitages wrapped round by the hills dot the landscape. Every cabin has its own name. Besides Shanti Peace they are designated as: Transfiguration, Our Lady of Solitude and Fidelis. Each is simply furnished, but unlike fifteen years ago, the dwellings have plumbing and electric with enough work space so a person can live in them.

Time taught us our construction mistakes. Vinyl siding or treated wood panels had to be installed because woodpeckers feasted on the old untreated lumber. Underpinning was attached. Possum fights and dead critter smells beneath the cabin floors could unnerve and nauseate any-one. Eaves were sealed up. Flying squirrels managed to get between the roof and the ceilings and scamper end-lessly overhead in the wee hours of the morning. It was enough to make a gal go berserk! One night I put a hole in the ceiling with the broom handle trying to discourage their escapades. No luck: simply had to chalk it all up to challenges of country life.

Suspended from an outside wall of each cabin, a bird house attracts many colorful feathered species. Near or attached to every hermitage is a shed for storing supplies, especially the wood that gets stashed away for the cold, short days and long nights of winter.

When Barbara was here she had a salt block outside her place and each morning she set out seven small piles of cracked corn for "her" deer to feast on. If anyone threatened to hurt them they would have to endure Barbara's ire. I would come down the mountain path in the old ATV (all terrain vehicle), and would they move? No! They'd look at me as if to say: "This is our space and you can just go around us."

One fall morning; it was the first day of deer season for hunting bucks. Of course the whole county is geared up for it. The kids have no school. Local dealers have just about sold all their stock pile of equipment and gear. The hunters were out before the crack of dawn seated in their preferred perches or on their selected sites waiting to spot a rack (an antlered deer). It was about 8:00 am and I was sitting quietly at the kitchen table. Looking out the window, three feet away I spied a 4 point buck casually eyeing me before quietly sauntering up the road in the direction of the chapel. Guess he knew he was within the realms of a peaceable kingdom.

Two tabby cats mind the mice around here. One feline is Dominique, who is dominated by the other; Lickety Split. A long time ago I had read that hermits of old were permitted to have a cat and had wondered why a cat rather than a dog. Try living in an old country cabin and the reason quickly becomes apparent. Tiny rodents squeeze into the smallest, least drafty places, propagate and inundate the premises in no time. A good feline is a priceless commodity and a warm fuzzy besides.

Many people have crossed the thresholds of this place in Colt Run Hollow and continue to do so. Some have come for many years, some for months and others for weeks and days. All have arrived searching for a deeper wisdom, closer union with their Creator, or something that will lighten their way as they spend the days of their lives here on the planet. All have come looking for time to just "be" and to sink into the womb of nature and feel the embrace of an all loving God.

One such person was Edessa and she appeared on my hermitage doorstep one early October day. At age 17 she was absolutely certain she was meant to spend two and a half months alone, in a solitary cabin, high on the mountain, in these West Virginia woods. I was not so certain. She looked like a typical teenager, who was atypical in her pursuit. Edessa's shoulder length brown hair was pulled back and banded. Streaks of brightly dyed, fuchsia, colored strands mingled with her natural brown ones. Cell phone and Apple Computer in-tow, she wore slim-line black jeans, a blue scoop neck blouse, and a black cardigan manufactured by Gap. Purple flip-flops flapped at her heels while her young, round, pink, pimpled-face glowed with eagerness to start the adventure.

I had e-mailed months before asking just why she wanted to do this and asking for some references from teachers, and other adults. She had replied: "I am not sure what I want to do with my life yet. I need a sense of direction. I graduated from high school early because some of those four years were home-schooled and had me ahead of other kids in my studies. It doesn't seem right to spend my parent's money foolishly at a university. I'd rather have an idea of what I want to do first. If I can get out into nature, be alone and listen for the voice of the Spirit, I think I'll discover what path to take."

In the mail had come references from teachers and mentors that were very affirming of this movement in her life. With some reservations, I said to myself: "I bet more parents would welcome some of this reflective musing in their offspring! Edessa certainly deserves a chance and seems mature beyond her years. Given the worst case scenario, I could always call her mom to come and get her if it doesn't work out."

Her father was a CEO of a large business firm and her mother was a psychologist in upstate New York. Delphi had driven her here, along with provisions which were all stuffed into a tiny, tan Toyota. Edessa was her only daughter. The couple had a son studying over in Fribourg, Germany. Now with Edessa attempting to discover her own path in the wide world, this step away from the family nest was causing her dear mom an emotional upheaval. The mother's eyes glistened with tears. She was not the least bit eager to leave her daughter behind in, what some might term a precarious situation.

We sat in the main house kitchen for a few moments for refreshments and questions from mom like: "Will the cell phone work up there? Does it get really cold? How do you heat the place? Is the lock on the door sturdy? Are there any dangerous animals, like coyotes or black bears in the woods? Just how far away is this main house from her cabin? Do you have 911 here?" Meanwhile, Edessa is fidgeting in the chair, chomping at the bit and dying to see her hermitage.

Twenty minutes later with major fears allayed and confirmation that I hadn't seen any ferocious animals in the woods in thirty-two years here on the property, we began the transfer of stuff from the Toyota to the Nissan 4WD pickup. Cartons of books with authors names like Rilke, Nietsche, and Adams came first, then the huge sketch pad, followed by mostly dried foodstuffs, a few clothes, a white quilt, three pillows, a revolving shade meditation lamp, blow dryer, digital camera and…all things necessary for life in a forest.

The truck bed loaded, Edessa climbed onto the tiny, black, upholstered seat of the extend-cab and sat scrunched there while Mom hoisted herself up into the front passenger position. I turned the ignition on, and switched the gears to low four-wheel drive for our ascent up the red clay, mud-rutted mountainside. A few minutes and forward lurches later we arrived at the site.

From the front, the hermitage looked like a tiny Chinese pagoda with wide double glass doors and slightly pitched crown. From the back it resembled an Appalachian hunting cabin with a huge window facing a grove of hickory trees. Once inside the back door, Edessa exclaimed: "This is PERFECT! It is exactly the right size and what I wanted." Delphi looked quizzical and just shrugged her shoulders. One corner held a small, cast iron, rectangle shaped, heating stove and a timber box loaded with kindling. There was a kitchenette area, an old pea-green colored recliner, a desk, table and a chair. Hidden behind a drape in the far right corner was a shower cubicle and commode. A ladder hung on two nails and was used for accessing the loft containing a window facing the rising sun. The pagoda part of the hermitage held an armoire for her stuff, a night stand and a bed where a person could lay and look out over the woods to see all of Mother Nature's moods. Another exclamation issued forth from Edessa: "This is where I am supposed to be!"

Delphi stayed the night up there with her daughter in the cabin. She nestled in a sleeping bag spread atop a piece of rubber foam and then rose early the next morning to begin the long journey back to New York. After gathering her daughter in a big bear hug, and choking back tears, she descended the mountain and steered her empty Toyota homeward.

Edessa could have used a warm fuzzy and was provided one. A few days before her arrival someone just happened (as often happens around here), to casually drop off a tiny, cuddly female kitten by the chapel door. Purr-snickety was a soft gray colored feline with tan eyes, a gentle disposition, oodles of energy, and a purr like a well-tuned motor. Since the two other cats already had a home at the main house and eschewed any more company Purr-snickety attached herself in no time to Edessa. She spent the nights balled up between her keeper's chest and abdomen and by day romped the woodlands at her heels.

Hours passed into days, and the days into weeks as Edessa grew acclimated to the nest in nature she had discovered. There was time just to "be." Hours were hers to savor. She could read, write, sketch, relax, roam and most of all, observe and listen. She didn't have to put a "face" on for anyone, or meet expectations, or get anywhere on time. She could almost see things grow and her sense of hearing became attuned to the slightest rustling movement. Sun drenched dawns, starlit nights, leaves dappled in red, orange and gold hues, lent a kaleidoscopic canopy of color to enfold her as she peered out the windows, sat on the porch, or hiked long winding solitary trails in the woods.

As the days and nights ran together the concept of time vanished. Edessa began absorbing some of the mysterious ways of nature. A sense of the Absolute and the all pervading pulse of the universe penetrated her soul. As new insights seeped in other maxims displaced ideas her previous world vision held sacrosanct. She asked herself: "What is truly important? What is worth putting my energy into? The fast track of modern life – is it a road to nowhere? How much do I really need to be happy and at peace? From this vantage point I require nothing much at all; a few clothes, a little roof over my head, simple food, free space to stretch and grow in mentally, physically, and spiritually. My real hunger is to be submerged in the vastness of the Infinite and be propelled from within by wonder, and gratitude."

Occasionally, as the last shades of sunset dipped out of sight the cell phone rang. One evening Corrie, a dear friend, called saying: "How can you take all that quiet space?" What is happening with you?" Edessa replied: I'm just fine. I love this time. I'm here grappling with life decisions; the ones I make in the near future are going to profoundly affect my life and set its direction. I don't want to make huge mistakes if I can help it. I'm just not in a hurry to go to college. Maybe I'll just get some odd jobs, travel a bit and learn more about the world and its people. I don't care about amassing possessions." Corrie had much to think about that night after the conversation ended and her friend Edessa, on a far distant mountain, stared out at the stars and witnessed a sliver of a crescent moon as it slid behind the hickory trees.

Edessa did not stay for the two and a half months as originally intended but she did stay a full month which I felt was remarkable for one as young as she. I asked her before she left if she found what she had come for and with a wondrous smile that spread across her youthful face, she exclaimed: "Yes!"

For the first time in twenty-seven years I have spent the winter alone here on the grounds. At first I was really dismayed and wondered why God was not sending others to stay. Then winter neared its end. I'd been given time to sink more deeply into the quiet surrounded by the snowy whiteness of glistening landscapes, of barren trees on rolling hills, of sunlit, then star-studded skies. In the profound silence of the days and nights I grew accustomed again to the rhythm of my very first years here when the Spirit propelled me into the wilderness to speak to my heart. The whole scenario reminded me of what my spiritual director had once said: "A contemplative has to go up the mountain alone." In essence we are called to follow a different drummer; One that beckons us on to things unseen. What at first seemed like a deep sorrow turned into a quiet joy and time of union with God.

In the solitude as I pray the hours of the Office, sit in quiet meditation, go about doing the manual labor, or writing, there is a definite consciousness of "being with" other sisters and brothers who are praying and living the same type of life all over our world. We too make up the "body of Christ." In a world where so often might seems to make right, when what material things a person possesses makes for importance, when busyness and competition are of the essence, the solitary is on earth to sing a new, yet ancient song, to proclaim praise, to give thanks, to petition, and to adore.

Many years ago Bishop Bernard Schmitt, the head of our diocese at that time, came here to the holler and presided at a public ceremony in the little chapel. He conferred upon me the irrevocable, Solemn Rite of Consecration to a Life of Virginity. The Rite goes way back to the first centuries of Christianity, predating any establishment of religious communities. A prayer in the ritual states: "O Lord, be Yourself, her glory, her joy, her whole desire. Be her comfort in sorrow, her wisdom in perplexity, her protection in the midst of injustice, her patience in adversity, her riches in poverty, her food in fasting, her remedy in time of sickness. She has chosen you above all things; may she find all things in possessing You."

A person would have to be out of their mind to think they could embrace this type of life alone without the blessing and help of the Lord. With that help it is a joy beyond the power of expression.

Sometimes outside the walls of the hermitage, in the far off distance I hear the faint grating sound of an up-shifting eighteen wheeler, or the whirring blades of a helicopter making for a hospital helipad. The sounds can pull me out of my moment's reverie and bring to mind what some call, the "real" world; the culture of our day.

In my family there was an in-law who could not abide silence. Some sort of entertainment always had to be engaged in. If the Bose wasn't blaring, the TV, the computer, music CD, or DVDs were. He was very well known by others but very ill at ease with himself. Busy from daylight to dark — I suppose most people would say he lived in the real world. He appeared to be incapable of inhabiting his own inner space in peace. For many folks these days all these distractions are common occurrences. However when a person is afraid to be quiet, I think it speaks of a deep dissonance within them. They resemble a rapidly moving freight train that isn't going to be able to negotiate the next sharp curve; the next great crisis in life.

A couple of years ago I witnessed people at an airport terminal rushing along the level moving walkways as they practically bounded from one destination to the next. Brief cases, laptops, and luggage in tow with one hand while a cell phone clamped against the ear occupied the other. On the airplane, out came the iPods, the blackberries, headsets, and laptops. Few people spoke to the person seated next to them.

Who hasn't noticed the crazed daze of faces in retail stores as some people scurry around before the holidays trying to get the best last minute deals on merchandise? Who has not known parents working multiple jobs so their children can have many commodities but not those gifts which they need most, tender love and attention. They certainly are not evil people but they seem to be caught up in a whirling centrifuge. Life is so fast and at least many think it has to be that way to allow them to enjoy the 'good life.'

One day a letter came from an editor of a magazine in California asking for an "inspiring" piece of writing and then she said to me: "Don't think a lot of people out here aren't fed up with the present culture." She meant by that, the fast paced expediency of daily life, the shallowness, superficiality, and lack of in-depth vision of those around her.

I cannot speak for the larger towns in West Virginia; those like Morgantown, Charleston, Clarksburg or Parkersburg. However, ensconced in the state's hill and country hollows many folks inhabit their little patch of earth and live a hidden existence. The term 'hermit' is really not a rarity if it can be stretched to mean a person who is pensive, prayerful and who spends their day doing simple manual labor. These solitary folks cloistered by the hills, who pass most of their time by themselves, are often welcoming and loving to those who cross their thresholds (in peace). They have been mentors to me. Many have a sense of balance, a joy of spirit and a peace that radiates from them. Their priorities seem to be right on target. The things of earth are beautiful and delight the eye but they are passing away. They know this. Only love remains. Simon Tugwell OP said it so well: "We must allow ourselves, as honestly as we can, to be challenged by the reality of God's world, as it seeps through the cracks in our home-made world, and so gradually learn to trust in him, and so to love him, and so to become docile to his creating and his commanding." Most of the elderly that I have cared for, without knowing it have incarnated Tugwell's thought.

There are some people in our state who burn with indignation when they hear the term "hillbillys," applied to residents. All the nuances that term implies such as rustic living without running water, plumbing, electric, modern appliances, lack of education, and so on is enough to cause their caustic remarks. There are pockets of privation in our state but the vast majority of folks have modern utilities and at least basic education. Along with these many have an intense love for the land and are gifted with amazing creativity. This creative genius is especially evident at Tamarack, a center near Beckley that displays the magnificent work of artisans from all over the state.

Pastures may look better and greener on the other side of state boundaries where educational facilities and economic opportunities are more in abundance. One could not deny that jobs are crucial and that there is a scarcity of them in parts of our state. The other side of the scene though is not always more beneficial. I lived and worked in two of the biggest cities in our country: Chicago and Pittsburgh. For years, I was immersed in those metropolises where the seething squalor, loud noise and often skewed, debased drug /alcohol induced cravings of many people around me suffocated my spirit. The poor of the city are far more bereft of comfort and a sense of well-being than the poor of the country. The latter have the space of green earth on which to see plants grow, bright star-spangled, night sky domes, mountain vistas and water courses, all bathed in the silence of creation to soothe their spirits. For inner city folks much of life is lived in a concrete jungle with noisy clamor, substance addictions, prostitution and destitution. I have seen Appalachians move into that culture shrivel up and die.

Many West-Virginians realize that they have something to offer that super-cedes power and monetary gain. An ancient wisdom penetrates this place and neighbors care about each other. On the main thoroughfares coming into the state the governor promoted and posted a sign that read: "Welcome to West Virginia – Open for Business." A state wide clamor had it reversed and by popular demand

it reads: "Welcome to West Virginia, Wild and Wonderful."
Does that not speak for how the indigenous view their terrain and environs?

Maybe fast-paced successful entrepreneurs could learn something from those who wiggle their toes on grassy dew-drenched slopes, or stand in rapt wonder as a fireball sun crests over a distant horizon. Life might be hard here in some places but it also can and does spark creativity among our artisans. They may not be well-to-do but many do well with the modest lives they have carved out in these hills. While laziness is just as reprehensible as greedy capitalism when the last mile is traveled and the last race run, what will have really mattered? How much income we've made, or how many IRAs we can claim? How sumptuous our dwellings were or how fashionably we were dressed?

The Word tells us that it is those who have loved, adored, praised their Creator and cared about their neighbor who will be blessed.

Before each of us reaches the end of our days and our true homeland we will have to enter at least into the solitude of the heart and be dispossessed not only of material creation but, even those things that our egos cling to like pride, self-importance, and all attachments. We all have to go through the dark valley alone to become little once again, so small that we are easy to handle, so empty that we can be filled with Light, so self-abandoned we can be taken into the joy of God. I would just like to say: "I believe it will be easier to do it after having lived in the hollers and among the folks of West Virginia."

email: mcnulty.jeanne@gmail.com
copies available at Amazon.com

LaVergne, TN USA
22 July 2010
190389LV00008B/9/P